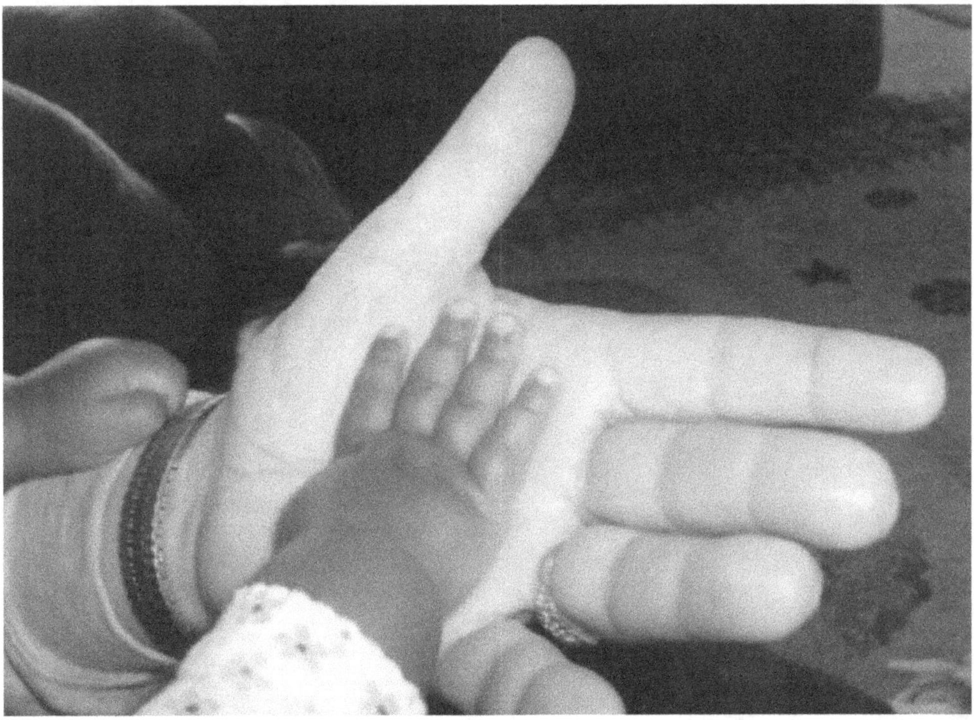

" . . . BLESSED ARE THEY
WHO PUT THEIR TRUST IN HIM."

PSALM 2:12

John Gillette's writings flow from a lifetime of experience. It is one thing to write out of a knowledge based on research. It is an entirely different thing to write out of a depth of life experience. John has both. As a pastor who has cared for the needs of a congregation, as a husband who has experienced the tragic loss of a wife, and as a child of God who has walked through the joys and pain of following the Lord, John has so much to offer in this series. From the opening pages, through to the very end, you will be blessed by the insights, loving tone and encouragement you receive from this series. God has used John greatly in ministry and will continue to use him through this life-giving series.

—Josh Mateer, D. Min.

True, illustrative, practical stories are like windows that unlock Bible truths and promises. Along with masterfully orchestrated short stories should come the truth that God's word and love has been experienced by His servants as they partner with Him in the work of rebuilding the Kingdom. A gifted teacher, Dr. Gillette lives an ordinary life abiding in Christ and being an obedient servant of the Lord. As he sees God working in his life, and in the lives of those to whom he ministers, his faith is refreshed and he is encouraged to press on through life's uncertainties.

Only a lifetime dedicated to nurturing, ministering, teaching, and keen insight through the power of the Holy Spirit, can produce such poignant stories that teach and challenge.

—Mulonge M. Kalumbula, Ph.D.

John's books give us hope and light. He reminds us that through Jesus we are never alone. I have certainly needed that reminder in my life and my practice. In holding a patient's hand, and helping them through a condition or disease, reminding them that they are never alone has become the greatest gift of health care.

—Linda M. Kunce, D.C.

The series reminds me that Jesus knows what it's like to live in a human body. I have received Jesus and his forgiveness, but as the book suggests, I also have power from the Holy Spirit. His books have encouraged me to gain courage through prayer and confidence in Jesus to meet my needs. John's honesty is very special to read as he reflects on his own life and struggles. I like his explanation that "the soul is where the emotions are and the mind is where the thinking takes place." It's been good for me to read that God works through weakness, and learn that John found God with him in the middle of the struggles.

—*Arvid W. Vandyke, Ed.D.*

Discovering *God's Counsel* is a book full of great spiritual truths from someone who has developed a very close and deep relationship with Jesus through his life. John provides a meaningful and inspirational testimony, with examples from his own experiences, of how relying on God's Word and promises can give you power, hope, and peace you need to overcome life's struggles and challenges. The Scriptures he chose in his book were on point and helpful. It was an enjoyable and wonderful read.

—*Thoa Reyna, J.D.*

John has written a user-friendly and practical series for anyone desiring to live beyond the superficial and venture into the supernatural. The world needs this *Pastoral Health Care Series*. Pastors and followers of Jesus need the insights from John's lifetime experience of walking with God and caring for His people through the power of the Holy Spirit. John has brilliantly show that God is enough, God's love is real, God's counsel is enduring, and God reigns supremely. This important series will serve both the church and the world for many years to come.

—*Kizombo Kalumbula, Jr., Ph.D.*

John Gillette's inspirational book *Glorify God* is a fantastic reminder of how I should approach each day and how blessed I am. It is so easy to get caught up in the hustle and bustle of today's lifestyle and forget what is really important. John's encouraging words are a great reminder of how we all should live each day. I have a great foundation of faith nut John's book helps me to remember what is important and allows me to reflect on the wonderful things I have and to be gracious to God for those blessings.

—*Tammy Thelen, Au.D., CCC-A*

Note from the Author

I believe in God's sovereignty and compassion. I am learning to let go of self and to hold onto someone that can do whatever he pleases. Sometimes life is cruel, sometimes it is full of suffering, physically and psychologically. A spiritual solution to meet difficult trials has become my goal. God's word carries with it no uncertainties. I want it to saturate my mind and heart.

The *Pastoral Health Care* series and Divine Dialogue series was created through unexpected heart disease (open heart surgery), cancer (medication and surgery), a stroke and major head injury after a car accident that also resulted in the death of my wife.

It is helping me to develop an adequate level to supernatural, psychological and physical adjustments. It may help you as well. It has brought me security.

—*John F. Gillette, Ph.D., D. Min.*

Satisfying
STRENGTH

Books by John Gillette:

Discovering God's Sufficiency
Going Beyond Ourselves and Experiencing the Supernatural
Pastoral Health Care — Part One

Discovering God's Love
Confirming God's Love through the evidence of historical facts
Pastoral Health Care — Part Two

Discovering God's Counsel
Applying his spiritual solution to meet difficult trials
Pastoral Health Care — Part Three

Discovering God's Kingdom
Finding a way to understand ourselves in a complex world
Pastoral Health Care — Part Four

Discovering God's Heart
Finding God's heart pulse is our daily challenge
Pastoral Health Care — Part Five

Glorify God
Christianity is a divine vitality
Divine Dialogue — Part One

Dynamic Doer
Biblical Christianity is Jesus Christ
Divine Dialogue — Part Two

Satisfying Strength
Biblical meditation works. Allow Psalms to sweep you into all directions.
Divine Dialogue—Part Three

Discipling Dynamics
Christian counseling teaching tool.
Divine Dialogue — Part Four

Triplets Trilogy
A spiritual autobiography of praise, promise and prayer.
Divine Dialogue — Part Five

*Biblical meditation works.
Allow Psalms to sweep you
into all directions.*

DIVINE
DIALOGUE
PART 3

Satisfying
STRENGTH

"HE THAT DWELLETH IN THE SECRET PLACE
OF THE MOST HIGH SHALL ABIDE UNDER THE
SHADOW OF THE ALMIGHTY."

PSALM 41:1

JOHN F. GILLETTE
Teaching Pastor, Pastoral Health Care Ministries
WITH JOY E. GILLETTE

Chapbook Press

Schuler Books
2660 28th Street SE
Grand Rapids MI 49512

www.schulerbooks.com/chapbook-press

Satisfying Strength

Copyright ©2021 — Dr. John F. Gillette, Ph.D., D. Min.
All rights reserved. Published 2021.
Printed at Schuler Books, Chapbook Press, Grand Rapids, Michigan, in the United States of America.

Distribution contact:at jjgillette@comcast.net.

ISBN 13: 978-1-948237-87-1

Library of Congress Control Number: 2021914833

Typist: Michael Sharp
Cover Design: Frank Gutbrod Graphic Design

Printed in the United States of America

*I appreciate Dr. Linda M. Kunce and
her spiritual, psychological, physiological
adjustments for my struggles.
I love her insights in my recent publication
Satisfying Strength — Pastoral Health Care.
I respect her professional patient consideration
in knowledge, sensitivity, passion and work.*

It is with great affection that I dedicate this book series to my wife, Joy, who radiates God's grace. We wrote the Pastoral Health Care Series together.

Applying God's spiritual solutions to meet us in difficult trials has become even more practical in my life with the recent death of my dear wife, Joy. This book has been reproduced in her memory. While the content is the same, my dedication has become more personal than ever before. The separation is painful but as I gather my suffering and feelings of incompleteness, I will succeed with God's peace and presence. The guidelines of this book have brought blessing to our life together. We have pursued them with great persistence. I am assured that she is in God's presence, rejoicing and at peace. I will be with her to experience God's eternal presence someday as well.

". . . blessed are they who put their trust in Him."
Psalm 2:12

Table of Contents

INTRODUCTION | 1

Psalm 1:1-2	Counsel	8
Psalm 2:4	Laughter	10
Psalm 3:3-4	Shield	12
Psalm 4:1	Prayer	14
Psalm 5:1	Meditation	16
Psalm 6:9	Weeping	18
Psalm 7:10	Defense	20
Psalm 8:1	Excellent	22
Psalm 9:1-2	Wonders	24
Psalm 10:1	Indifference	26
Psalm 11:1	Trust	28
Psalm 12:1	Help	30
Psalm 13:5	Trusted	32
Psalm 14:1	Fool	34
Psalm 15:1	Dwelling	36
Psalm 16:8	Confidence	38
Psalm 17:5	Path	40
Psalm 18:1-3	Strength	42
Psalm 19:1	Creator	44
Psalm 20:1; 21:13	Affirmation	46
Psalm 22:8	Salvation	48

Psalm 23:6	Direction	50
Psalm 24:1	Rule	52
Psalm 25-32	Teach	54
Psalm 33-39	Fear	56
Psalm 40:8	Substitution	58
Psalm 40:4	Delight	60
Psalm 41:11	Blessed	62
Psalm 42:1-2	Panteth	64
Psalm 43:5	Hope	66
Psalm 44:4	King	68
Psalm 45:2	Power	70
Psalm 46:1	Refuge	72
Psalm 47:9	Proclamation	74
Psalm 48-49	Guidance	76
Psalm 50:1-6	Judge	78
Psalm 51:10	Sin	80
Psalm 52:8	Mercy	82
Psalm 53:1	Deceived	84
Psalm 54:4	Helper	86
Psalm 55:17	Communication	88
Psalm 56:3	Faith	90
Psalm 57:7	Steadfast	92
Psalm 58:11	Reward	94
Psalm 59:1	Defend	96
Psalm 60:6	Holy Part 1	98
Psalm 60:6	Holy, Part 2	100
Psalm 61, 62	Suffering	102

Psalm 63, 64	Seek | 104
Psalm 65, 66	Supplication | 106
Psalm 67, 68	Submission | 108
Psalm 69:30	Song | 110
Psalm 70:1-5	Awesome | 112
Psalm 71:1-24	Sovereign | 114
Psalm 72:1-20	Deeds | 116
Psalm 73:1-28	Guide | 118
Psalms 80-83	Shine | 120
Psalms 84-89	Favorites | 122
Psalm 90:1-17	Generations | 124
Psalm 91:1-16	Abide | 126
Psalm 100:1-5	Serve | 128
Psalm 101:1-8	Blameless | 130
Psalm 102:1-28	Cry | 132
Psalm 103:1-22	Magnify | 134
Psalm 104:1-35	Meditations | 136
Psalm 105:1-45	Acts | 138
Psalm 106:1-48	Remember | 140
Psalm 107:1-43	Thanksgiving | 142
Psalm 111:1-10	Respect | 144
Psalm 113: 1-9	Praise | 146
Psalm 116:1-19	Call | 148
Psalm 117:1-2	Faithful | 150
Psalm 119:1-8	Revelation | 152
Psalm 119:9-16	Obey | 154
Psalm 119:17-24	Slander | 156

Psalm 119:25-32	Preserve | 158
Psalm 119:33-40	Instruction | 160
Psalm 119:41-48	Love | 162
Psalm 119:49-56	Thankful | 164
Psalm 119:57-64	Master | 166
Psalm 119:65-72	Good | 168
Psalm 119:73-80	Word | 170
Psalm 119:81-88	Faint | 172
Psalm 119:89-96	Anchor | 174
Psalm 119:97-104	Passion | 176
Psalm 119:105-112	Keep | 178
Psalm 119:113-120	Hallelujah | 180
Psalm 119:121-128	Discernment | 182
Psalm 119:129-136	Light | 184
Psalm 119:137-144	Righteous | 186
Psalm 119:145-152	Communion | 188
Psalm 119: 153-160	Promise | 190
Psalm 119:161-168	Rejoice | 192
Psalm 119:169-176	Positive | 194
Psalm 134:1-3	Worship | 196
Psalm 145:1-21	Exaltation | 198
Psalm 150:1-6	Trumpet | 200

ACKNOWLEDGEMENTS | 202

ABOUT THE AUTHOR | 203

Introduction

Meditation 1

The Bible says, "Speak to yourselves in psalms, and hymns, and spiritual songs, singing and making melody in your hearts to the Lord." (Ephesians 5:19). In the Christian life, the Psalms should always be a special blessing. Psalm 1 has been a favorite. I have gone to the first three verses of this Psalm many times. "Blessed is the man that walkest not in the counsel of the ungodly, nor standeth in the way of sinners, not sitteth in the seat of the scornful; but his delight is in the law of the Lord; and in his law doth he meditate day and night. And he shall be like a tree planted by the rivers of water that bringeth forth his fruit in his season; his leaf also shall not wither; and whatsoever he doeth shall prosper." (Psalm 1:1-3).

From these verses we see the importance of the believer's meditating on the Scriptures. The Amplified Bible renders verse two: "But his delight and desire are in the law of the Lord and on His law — the precepts, the instructions, and teachings of God." We are to think on the

Scriptures during the day and even the night time when we are awake.

When we do this, we will be fruitful and grow to maturity like a tree planted by water. The Bible says, "Every scripture is God-breathed, given by His inspiration and profitable for instruction, for reproof, for correction of error and discipline in obedience, and for training in righteousness."

This is what the Word of God is and does. No believer can live an effective spiritual life without it. It was Jesus who said, "It is the spirit that quickeneth; the flesh profiteth nothing. The words that I speak unto you, they are the spirit and the life." (John 6:63). Because the Word of God is so important to our spiritual lives, our spiritual effectiveness depends on our maintaining a daily time of meditating on the Scriptures. Let us center our thoughts on the Word of God. The results will be simply a reproduction of the Bible in our lives.

Meditation 2

The Bible says, "And he reasoned in the synagogue . . . and persuaded the Jews and Greeks . . . and he continued teaching the word of God among them" (Acts 18:4,11). I know of no other way to give the

Introduction

authority of the Scriptures than to continue teaching the word. I would like to reason and persuade you but the Scripture is a living, vital agency with supernatural power in itself. Read the promise. "For as the rain cometh down and the snow from heaven, and returneth not thither, but watereth the earth, and maketh it bring forth and bud, that it may give seed to the sower, and bread to the eater: so shall my word be that goeth forth out of my mouth; it shall not return unto me void, but it shall accomplish that which I please, and it shall prosper in the thing whereto I sent it"(Isaiah 55:10,11). To the same purpose Jeremiah has written, "Is not your word like a fire? saith the Lord; and like a hammer that breaketh the rock in pieces?: (Jeremiah 23:29). God uses His wording — "For the word of God is quick (living), and powerful (active) and sharper than any two-edged sword, piercing even to the dividing asunder of soul and spirit, and of the joints and marrow and is the discerner of the thoughts and intents (ideas) of the heart" (Hebrews 4:12).

The Bible is an ancient book for modern times. It is one book, one history, one story and one mind produced it. God Himself became a man so that we might know what to think of when we think of

God (John 1:14, 14:9). I could give all the evidences for scriptural authority, but why don't you read the Bible for yourself and let it prove itself.

Meditation 3

The Bible says, "As newborn babes, desire the sincere milk of the word that ye may grow thereby" (I Peter 2:2). God has given his word so that believers may grow thereby. We haven't fulfilled our obligations to the word until application has taken place. The Bible is not only the source book for information but has life-changing power for today. Growth in the spiritual life comes not merely from hearing but from hearing and doing. The Bible says, "the effectual doer shall be blessed in what he does" (James 1:25). If you know these things, you are blessed if ye do them (John 12:17).

The Bible has been given so that man's basic nature can be changed. "All Scripture is given by God and is profitable for teaching, for reproof, for correction, for training in righteousness, that the man of God may be adequate, equipped for every good work" (II Timothy 3:16,17). It teaches, rebukes, restores, trains for righteous living. It equips us to do the work that God wants us to do. The Bible convicts,

Introduction

regenerates, nurtures, cleanses, counsels, guides, prevents sin, revives, strengthens, gives wisdom, delivers, and helps. The Bible alone realistically and sufficiently meets man's deepest problems, longings, needs, and inadequacies. It provides the answers to man's need for deliverance from the penalty of sin, for spiritual progress, daily victory, for guidance and personal relationships, and conduct. As we learn the Scriptures, let us apply it to our daily activities.

Meditation 4

The Bible says, "Blessed are the undefiled in the way, who walk in the law of the Lord" (Psalm 119:1). What is wrong with reading the Bible? Why do people think it is so strange? Some people have the idea that the Bible is just for the mentally weak, some people think it is for the ignorant, some people imagine that it is only for the shut-ins, and some think that it is only for the children. Why do the teens, young adults turn from it? I believe they do not go on to read it or believe it or study it or follow it. If we are going to walk in the law of the Lord, we must follow this pattern.

First, we need to study it through. That is, master a verse every day. Think of it; at the end of

Satisfying STRENGTH

the year, you will have 365 verses in your heart and in your mind to bring about happiness, direction, peace, and contentment. We need to pray about it. We must let each verse become a part of our very being, praying the verse right into reality, and then seeing the promises of God as we claim them to change our lives. We must write down our thoughts. We cannot remember everything but our computer mind has it and we need to refresh our memory. That, of course, brings us to working it out. Let the Bible get in our heart and then live it out every day. It is not good only to study it through or pray about it or put it down or work it out, but we must also pass it on. We must talk about it. Let the Word of God inspire and bless your heart. It takes discipline. You cannot be lazy. Walk in the Law of the Lord and you will find purpose and peace.

Counsel
PSALM 1:1-2

Primary Text
Repeat the text:

"Blessed is the man that walketh not in the counsel of the ungodly . . . But his delight is in the law of the Lord; and in his law doth he meditate day and night."

Personal Response
Remember the text

The word *blessed* refers to happiness. This provides a firm foundation, passion, knowledge and practice. I thank God for giving me Christian parents that provided a firm foundation. I grew up with a passion for the Bible. Absolute knowledge has its foundation on God's intellect. With practice, we see the fruit of it. The law — scripture gives conviction, courage, and challenges. I believe in Almighty God.

Pondering Thoughts
Reflect on the Text

Delight means that I enjoy and have passion in God's word. *Law* means God's word. Meditation refers to thinking about the law. Pondering over it is a pleasure. I should spend day and night in the Holy Scriptures.

Practical Application
Respond to the text

I am challenged to apply God's word to my activities.
I affirm that the truth is in Jesus Christ.
I pray for a deeper passion in thinking God's way.
It is exciting to follow God's counsel.
Thinking with God's mind is spiritual meditation.

Laughter
PSALM 2:4

Primary Text
Repeat the text

"He that sitteth in the heaven shall laugh."

Personal Response
Remember the text

God's laughter is not from humor but from rebellion. His laughter is based upon man's foolishness. God loves humanity but hates stupidity. I experienced two times of laughter from groups of people, conservative and liberal. The first time, I was in my twenties being examined for ministry license. The laughter was given with contempt and insincerity to confuse me. The second occasion was my graduate doctoral exam on Religion. This was a group of educated unbelievers. They accepted my project defense. They accepted my defense but didn't agree with my subject.

Pondering Thoughts
Reflect on the text

God loves humanity but hates those foolish hearts. Rebellion comes from within. God brings understanding with the truth. We must choose. He is the giver of faith. Acceptance comes with belief. Belief comes with faith. Faith comes with a decision. Decision is our choice to follow Jesus Christ or not.

Practical Application
Respond to the text

I am more prepared for the enemy.
I expect laughter for doing good.
I recognize where the force of evil comes from.
I agree to disagree agreeably.
I am ready to follow up.

Shield

PSALM 3:3-4

Primary Text
Repeat the text

"But Thou, O Lord, art a shield for me . . . and the lifter up of my head."

Personal Response
Remember the text

My shield has protected me during my faith walk. God's Word is my shield. I discovered it in childhood in our children's Bible study, in my teenage gospel team, my college days in mission churches, and the list goes on. The *shield* was provided through *study* of God's word. This became my *sword* for defense. With a *sincere* heart, I could feel God's presence. The divine power became my constant helper. He lifted me to victory.

Pondering Thoughts
Reflect on the text

The shield became my protective armor. It began with Ephesians 6:17, the *sword* of the spirit. In Psalm 33:20, Jesus is my *helper*. In Psalm 51:12, God's *favor* is upon me. In Psalm 18:35, *salvation* is the way to relationship. In Psalm 91:4, the *truth* is my shadow in life. In Ephesians 6:16, *faith* will conquer the wicked. In Psalm 47:9, I am under the *exalted* one. I travel with courage because He lifts me up. I am surrounded with His Word.

Practical Application
Respond to the text

Every day, I am in God's Book. I learn to rely on what He says. I review when he has helped me in victories and discouragement. I rejoice when I remember. His favor has blessed me. I live with His shadow covering me. God my creator is with me. He has made a new creation out of me. I practice 1 Corinthians 10:13 in my life and discovered victory.

Prayer
PSALM 4:1

Primary Text
Repeat the text

"Hear me when I call . . . hear my prayer."

Personal Response
Remember the text

The word "call" caused my heart to want to pray more often. When we are in distress, we must learn to rest in God's arms. The quiet confidence is based upon being set apart. We are set apart to God. We are saved through Jesus Christ's blood. We have a relationship with the Holy Trinity. There is no fear; righteousness leads the way.

Pondering Thoughts
Reflect on the text

This chapter reveals the contrast between righteous and evil. The skeptic has no blessings. The righteous has a safe dwelling. Believers have been set apart and have the authority to pray. He will respond to us. I am complete in him (Colossians 2:9-10). He is over all principalities and powers (Colossians 2:9-10). He delivers me from evil (II Timothy 4:17-18). He helps me (Psalm 121:2-3). He is my strength (Psalm 73:25-26). When I call, he will respond.

Practical Application
Respond to the text

I am pleased that God hears me.
I am thankful that God provides confidence.
I am glad that God has called me into his family.
I am rejoicing that he gives guidance.
I am excited to follow his promises.

Meditation
PSALM 5:1

Primary Text
Repeat the text

"Give ear to my words, O Lord, consider my meditation."

Personal Response
Remember the text

Meditation is important. It brings us into a relationship with God. We discover truth. We find that he is dependable. We know that he is trustworthy. We learn that he is consistent. His word produces selflessness, fruitfulness and thanksgiving. Meditation will provide his perspective, understanding, and spiritual development.

Pondering thoughts
Reflect on the text

Biblical, spiritual meditation will provide right thinking. Righteousness will be my goal. I will seek it with an intense heart. This gives me purity in my path. His word will produce wisdom. Discipleship will be guided with discipline. God will consider my thoughts because they belong to him.

Practical application
Respond ot the text

The word of God is the right foundation.
The word of Christ is the right authority.
The word of His Spirit will be the right guidance.
The word of God will provide glory for himself, and blessing for me.

Weeping
PSALM 6:9

Primary Text
Repeat the text

"The Lord hath heard my supplication; The Lord will receive my prayer. Depart from me, all ye workers of iniquity . . ."

Personal Response
Remember the text

This text refers to a cry of repentance because of sin. Trial and sorrow produces brokenness of heart. The concern is rebuke without anger and chastening without wrath. God is touched with our infirmities and suffering. Jesus Christ knows what suffering is all about, without sin. He has suffered the cross for us that deserve it.

Pondering Thoughts
Reflect on the text

My requests have been granted. The Devil's crew can get lost. My enemies will disappear. In disgrace they will run from me. I can claim comfort and encouragement. In Christ's suffering and victory, we are winners.

Practical Application
Respond to the text

I face three enemies: the world, the flesh and the devil (Ephesians 2:1-3). Christ overcame the world (John 16:33, Galatians 6:14), and the flesh (Galatians 2:20, Romans 6:1-6), and the devil (Ephesians 1:19-23). I can be secure during my trials and temptations because victory has already been provided for me.

Defense
PSALM 7:10

Primary text
Repeat the text

"My defense is of God, which giveth the upright heart."

Personal Response
Remember the text

When in danger, in perplexity, or severe pain, "cry out to the Lord." He is our shelter, shield and savior. We will be delivered. Our defense is found in our uprightness in heart. We will experience divine interference. "O Lord my God, in thee do I put my trust. Save me from all them that persecute me, and deliver me." (Psalm 7:1).

Pondering Thoughts
Reflect on the text

The laws are grouped into two broad categories: man's relationship to God, and his relationship to the community. My focus will always be God and his will as it is recorded in his word. I shall have God before me. My character will reveal this relation in my life. My top focus will be to worship God in spirit and in truth.

Practical Application
Respond to text

My top focus will be complete trust in him in submissive labor. I shall have good family relationships. I will magnify in my life what I believe. I have value for human life. My top focus will be a lifelong relationship of commitment, trust, and a pure heart. I shall have absolute truth in all my decisions. My top focus will be an attitude of surrender to God which will provide peace and contentment. I like the word "shall" because it means with determination. I am consciously aware of the Holy Spirit's indwelling. As I practice the Law because of love:

> My character will reveal the defense.
> My value for human life will saturate decisions.
> My attitude will cause a sense of peace.

Excellent

PSALM 8:1

Primary Text

Repeat the text

"O Lord our Lord, how excellent is thy name in all the earth."

Personal Response

Remember the text

I am so glad that I can say "O Lord our God." I belong to him. I see his greatness every day. The very nature of God needs to be understood. He is infinite, absolute, unchangeable and perfect in all his ways. He is faithful (my doubt). He is holy (my sinfulness). He is love (my selfishness). He is truth (my falsehood). He has absolute knowledge (my questioning). He is all-powerful (my fear). He is everywhere (my presence). He is Lord (my disobedience). He is absolutely in control. He is excellent.

Pondering Thoughts
Reflect on the text

His perspective takes over, not my emotion or circumstances. My goal is "I will praise his name with my heart" (Psalm 86:12). I will model Christ's character through bearing fruit. My life will be saturated with His word. My foundation is faith. My motivation is found in love. My expectation is found in hope.

Practical Application
Respond to the text

Answer the questions with the Lord's excellent name behind each thought:

> Have I learned God's perspective?
> Do I practice faith in all my decisions?
> Do I practice love?
> Do I bear fruit?
> Do I practice God's promises?

Wonders

PSALM 9:1-2

Primary Text
Repeat the text

"I will show forth all thy wonders — deeds — marvelous work..."

Personal Response
Remember the text

The prophetic story of Psalms is continued in chapter nine and ending with the fifteenth. We get a glimpse of suffering and the man of sin (the lawless one). We see days of trials and testings. We will experience the Antichrist, the false messiah. We will also experience blessing and glory.

Pondering Thoughts
Reflect on the text

These words describe the deeds that God has accomplished for us:

Deliverance means to be set free. We may suffer but God will free us. He has prepared a victory path for us.

Restored means to reinstate. Sin has entered through rebellion anad disobedience. God has restored us through redemption.

Forgiveness is the activity of releasing us from the penalty of sin.

Spirit-filled is allowing God to be in charge of the will and being loyal to him.

Mercy means compassion given in love and provided through God's grace.

Judgement refers to making decisions based on God's justice.

Abide means to remain in God's instruction. God's intervention has taken place.

Practical Application
Respond to the text
Thank God for his marvelous works Biblically.
Review God's deeds in your personal life.
Remain firm in Holy Spirit confidence.

Indifference
PSALM 10:1

Primary Text
Repeat the text

"Why standest thou afar off, O Lord?"

Personal Response
Remember the text

"Lord, why are you so far away? Why do you hide yourself in times of trouble?" (Psalm 10:1, NIRV). "I trust in your faithful love. My heart is filled with joy because you will save me. I will sing to the Lord, He has been so good to me. (Psalm 10:3-6). The Lord is not indifferent. He cares. We must look at God's perspective. The chapter began with concern and defeat. If we live with affliction and darkness, God still is in charge. We must enter His presence with a sincere mind, and submissive heart.

Pondering Thoughts
Reflect on the text

God does not stand afar off. These chapters in Psalms speak of a prophetic picture. We see judgement and mercy. We see deliverance and restoration. Man's day is ended and the day of the Lord has begun. God has defeated the wicked one. The enemy: intellectual (Daniel 7:20), oratorical (7:20), political (11:21), commercial (8:25), military (8:24), administrative (13:1-2), and religious (2 Thessalonians 2:4).

Practical Application
Respond to the text

I must affirm God's compassion.
I must grow in God's discipleship.
I must continue in God's fellowship.
I must increase in God's service.
I must hear God's prompting.

Trust
PSALMS 11:1

Primary Text
Repeat the text

"In thee, O LORD, I put my trust."

Personal response
Remember the text

In times of persecution and danger, we can find safety. We live with unshaken faith that provides trust. We are able to rest in God's hands. Calmness is the result. Trust is defined by putting one's confidence in a thought, person, or thing. Thoughts come from words. "I trust God's word." (Psalm 119:44). I trust in the person of Jesus Christ. "My heart shall rejoice in him because we have trusted." (Psalm 33:21). He provides my needs. "I trust in the mercy of God." (Psalm 52:5).

Pondering Thoughts
Reflect on the text

Through trust these characteristics will flow from within our hearts:

I trust in His joy (Psalm 5:11).
I trust in His victory (Psalm 25:4,5).
I trust in His guidance (Psalm 3:5,6).
I trust in His blessing (Psalm 40:4,5).

Practical Application
Respond to the text

Through trust these characteristics will be demonstrated:

I trust in His deliverance (Psalm 22:4,5).
I trust in His goodness (Psalm 31:19).
I trust in His providence (Psalm 23:1).
I trust in His safety (Psalm 56:4,11).
In the last days faith, trust through obedience and submission will give us strength.

Help
PSALM 12:1

Primary Text
Repeat the text

"Help, Lord; for the godly are no more; for the faithful have vanished from among the children of men."

Personal Response
Remember the text

Holy men from God spoke as they were carried along by the Holy Ghost (2 Peter 1:21). Now, apostasy has taken place. Moral corruption is seen everywhere. It is creeping into our minds. The prayer is "Help, Lord" (v. 1). "Keep me from flattering lips" (v. 3). Help me not to depart from the truth. The prayer is *keep* me from apostasy.

Pondering Thoughts
Reflect on the text

The resource is God keeping me safe. "I will set him in safety." (v. 5). We don't have to abandon the truth. We can stay in God's gracious promises. Corruption doesn't have to corrupt me. God's pure word will work (v. 6). His word is unblemished. His word is loyal to the truth. His word is flawless and not divided. There will be no deliberate departure from God.

Practical Application
Respond to the text

I will be protected. "Thou shalt keep them" (v. 7). Righteousness will keep me safe. We may live in days of darkness but it will be overthrown.
The Lord will destroy flattering lips.
The Lord will help to provide safety.
The Lord will give wise guidance.
The Lord will keep me safe.

Trusted

PSALM 13:5

Primary Text
Repeat the text

"I have trusted in thy mercy; my heart shall rejoice in my salvation."

Personal Response
Remember the text

Deep suffering is found in verses 1-2. The soul is afflicted. How long do I have to suffer, Jehovah? Hear my cry for deliverance! The *struggle* may include discouragement, despair, depression, dejection. Please don't ignore me.

Pondering Thoughts
Reflect on the text

My soul can be *calm* through prayer (verses 3-4). Be concerned with my condition. Don't forsake me but hear my plea for assurance. My hope is expected from you. We can have assurance that you care. God's promise of fellowship is reassuring. Help me to look up.

Practical Application
Respond to the text

Victory is found in verses 5-6. Triumph will come. Deep despair can lead to the cry for a calm heart. Faith is the key. God knows us, sees us, hears us. I celebrate your rescue The cry, the calm will result in celebration

Fool
PSALM 14:1

Primary Text
Repeat the text

"The fool hath said in his heart, there is no God..."

Personal Response
Remember the text

This psalm is linked with the twelfth and thirteenth. Corruption and wickedness of the last days is seen. *Struggle* and agony of the godly is seen. Faith is the victory word through prayer that prevails.

The word 'fool' reveals the *depravity* of man's soul. Wickedness, moral corruption, evil, unwise thoughts based on the natural insight of man. The denial of a personal God is a lie against the consciousness of the human soul. The root to this madness is the human heart. The Antichrist exalteth himself above all that is called God. (2 Thessalonians 2:4).

Pondering Thoughts
Reflect on the text

Man is sinful and separated from God. Therefore, he cannot know and experience God's love and plan for his life. His self-will, characterized by an attitude of active rebellion or passive indifference is evidence of that the Bible calls 'sin.' (Romans 3:23, 6:23).

Practical Application
Respond to the text

Jesus Christ is God's only provision for man's sin. Through Him you can know and experience God's love and plan for your life. He died in our place (Romans 5:8). He rose from the dead. He appeared to more than five hundred (1 Corinthians 15:3-6). He is the only way to God (John 14:6). The fool can change and know God. Wisdom can be his rather than foolishness. Receive Jesus (John 1:12) through faith (Ephesians 2:8-9). New birth will bring a complete new person (John 3:1-8).

Dwelling
PSALM 15:1

Primary text
Repeat the text

"Lord, who shall abide in thy tabernacle? Who shall dwell on thy holy hill?"

Personal Response
Remember the text

The Lord demands practical righteousness yielded to his kingdom (Matthew 6:33). If we abide in Christ, we will dwell in his presence (John 15:4). We must live upright lives. We must learn to walk straight, act right, and tell the truth. We have to practice God's presence. We must learn to think like God by studying his word.

Pondering Thoughts
Reflect on the text

We must live blameless lives. We must understand evil and good. We have to be a good neighbor. We must be honest. We must learn to live in a glass house. Transformation is our priority.

Practical Application
Respond to the text

We must live respectable lives. We must recognize wrong beliefs and correct them. We must praise the follower of scripture. We must learn to disagree with respect. We must live steadfast lives.. We must learn to live unshaken lives. We must learn to practice what we believe. We must live in our secure faith.

Confidence
PSALM 16:8

Primary Text
Repeat the text

"I have set the Lord before me: because he is at my right hand, I shall not be moved."

Personal Response
Remember the text

"I have set the Lord before me." I have made a decision to *seek* the Lord with an earnest heart. He has become my *strength* in everything I do. He is my constant companion. In my inadequacy, I find strength and conviction. In Jesus Christ, I have moved from the negative to the positive. I am grateful to the Lord that his voice has been my passion for life.

Pondering Thoughts
Reflect on the text

"He is at my right hand." I belong to Him. I am his heir and have a great inheritance. I belong to his kingdom. I have a citizenship on earth and in heaven. He has given me faith. His strength flows into my bloodstream through the Holy Spirit. I exercise obedience and this gives me a reflection of Him. My *support* from him brings me joy.

Practical Application
Respond to the text

"I shall not be moved." I live in a contaminated world of sin. When it rubs off on me I conform and I develop a conscious communion with my Savior and Lord. I have a growing connection. In him I put my trust for eternity. In my super-sensitivity, I have discovered that I am secure in the Lord. I can say, "I shall not be moved." Steadfastness has become the fruit of strength and support.

Path

PSALM 17:5

Primary Text

Repeat the text

"Hold up my goings in thy paths, that my footsteps slip not."

Personal Response

Remember the text

This psalm is a prayer. The path is a divine intervention. Righteousness is the key to not failing; uprightness is the path to follow. How do I walk in an upright path? Do I have a genuine faith? I must keep my eyes upon the Savior who is "the author and finisher of our faith." (Hebrews 12:2). God's plan is that I have a firm *conviction* of faith. I have a personal *surrender* to God. Faith is a response of *trust* in a person, based upon that individual's character and word, which issues in *action*.

Pondering Thoughts
Reflect on the text

I will walk forward as I practice faith. I must make a *decision to accept* God's will and glorify him. The basis of faith is the Scriptures. The Bible is my source of strength. I *choose* to follow the word of God and practice his promises. *Faith is a union with* the Scripture. I cannot separate the true act of believing from that which is believed.

Practical Application
Respond to the text

Christ has given me faith. I can choose faith in trials, confusion, frustration and disappointment. I am a doer of God's word. The highest value in my life is spiritual.

My footsteps will not fail. Faith is Jesus' plan for me to succeed. Each thought will draw me closer to him.

Strength
PSALM 18:1-3

Primary Text
Repeat the text

"I will love thee, O Lord, my strength. The Lord is my rock and my fortress, and my deliverer: my God, my strength, on whom I will trust, my buckler, and the horn of my salvation, and my high tower.. I will call upon the Lord . . ."

Personal Response
Repeat the text

I come to the Lord for strength because of love. Love is a fundamental requirement for enlightenment. It is the highest motive or ground of moral action; Christian living is based upon it. "We love him because he first loved us." (1 John 4:19, 2 Corinthians 5:14, Romans 12:1-2). The intense emotion will bring strength. The following words will show how it works: I am strong and powerful through the Holy Spirit's empowerment.

Pondering Thoughts
Reflect on the text

My strength is solid because it starts with the Lord saying he is my rock. The Spirit of life flows from him to all who will drink (Exodus 17:6, John 4:13-14, 1 Corinthians 10:4). In the church Christ is the foundation (Matthew 16:18) and chief cornerstone (Ephesians 2:20).

My strength is solid and prepared for battle because Jesus is my fortress. He is my protection (Psalm 18:2, 31:3, 71:3). He is my defense and offensive weapon.

My strength is solid; it is sure and it separates me from the enemy. Christ delivers me. He releases me. I am on a win to win situation. Victory belongs to me because of the Lord Jesus Christ.

Practical Application
Respond to the text

This is a wonderful psalm. It is a record of marvelous deliverance, and of the victories which Jehovah has given. It is also a record of David's own heart, the truth of his affection toward God. We need to "call to the Lord" and be thankful for his strength, his love, his authority, his defense, his deliverance, his victory.

Creator
PSALM 19:1

Primary Text
Repeat the text

"The heavens declare the glory of God; and the firmament sheweth his handiwork."

Personal Response
Remember the text

The glory of God refers to his worth, to his power, to his excellence, to his greatness, to his holiness, to his divine manifestation and to his loving grace. His glory is the total of his essence and attributes. God's glory is seen in his creation handiwork. David focused on the heavens above him. There are many worlds in God's creation. They include the earth — plants and animals, on the ground, in the skies and on the waters. The human world: the rocks and crystals, worlds visible to the human eye and worlds so small and so far, we need special equipment to see them. There is insignificance when you start examining the heavens. Calculate distance in light years. Don't worship the creation but the Creator. He knows everything and maintains what he has made.

Pondering Thoughts
Reflect on the text

God's voice of power in creation prepares the way for his voice of grace. "The law of the Lord is perfect, converting the soul. The testimony of the Lord is sure, making wise the simple." (Psalm 19:7). The creator of creation wants a relationship with his creation. The heavens declare God's glory, and he wants to share in that glory. Through God's word, we become wise concerning salvation (2 Timothy 3:15). The word *simple* refers to childlike people who humbly receive God's truth (Matthew 11:25; Luke 10:21-24).

Practical Application
Respond to the text

"Yet to all who did receive him, to those who believed in his name, he gave the right to become children of God. . . " (John 1:12).

Affirmation
PSALM 20:1, PSALM 21:13

Primary Text
Repeat the text

"The LORD hear me in the day of trouble; the name of the God of Jacob defend me . . ." (Psalm 20:1).

"Be thou exalted, LORD, in thine own strength . . ." (Psalm 21:13

Personal Response
Remember the text

In chapter 20, we have a prayer before the battle. In chapter 21, we have victory. It is a plea for help and a response from God in trouble. We must learn to claim the promise of faith. "If God be for us, who can be against us?" (Romans 8:31). Our strength is not in us but in God. We must affirm God's sovereignty. God knows what to do and when to do it.

Pondering Thoughts
Reflect on the text

In chapter 20, we pray for help in trouble. In chapter 21, we are granted strength. Deliverance is found in the word "salvation." Take time to review victories. God reigns, we don't have to be afraid of the enemy. The declaration of faith is the control key. Simple trust will provide victory. Affirmation of faith will bring strength.

Practical Application
Respond to the text

Let us magnify the Lord. These two chapters go hand in hand. Weakness — strength, failure — deliverance, helplessness — victory. Exalt God's name. "These who honor me I will honor." (1 Samuel 2:30).

Salvation
PSALM 22:8

Primary Text
Repeat the text

"He trusted on the Lord that he would deliver him..."

Personal Response
Remember the text

This is a prophetic psalm. It speaks of Jesus Christ hanging between heaven and earth on the cross of Calvary. It is a description of his death. It is Jesus' trust and deliverance. His suffering was victorious. The seed in verse 30 is of service. We are to share God's grace. The message of the crucifixion will never grow old.

Pondering Thoughts
Reflect on the text

A genuine relationship with God comes through Jesus Christ. (Matthew 11:28-30). "Come unto me" is an open invitation. In verse 27 it is a divine initiative. The Holy Spirit convicts us. Jesus is the way initiated by the Father. Trying to save ourselves will not work. We have to recognize our sinful condition (Romans 3:23, 6:23, 5:8, 10:9-10).

Practical Application
Respond to the text

Work-based convictions will not be sufficient. We have to come to the end of our resources. Salvation in Jesus Christ includes an invitation to believe and surrender (2 Timothy 1:12).

The Father has chosen me, the Son has purchased me, and the Spirit has sealed me. I trust Jesus Christ. My job is to share that trust with others.

Direction
PSALM 23:6

Primary Text
Repeat the text

"Surely goodness and mercy shall follow me all the days of my life; and I will dwell in the house of the Lord forever."

Personal Response
Remember the text

I love little words like "me" and "my" that turn into important words of value for the believer to enjoy. The word "my" (my shepherd) turns into *relationship*. He protects me from danger, he literally lays his life on the line. He made himself my personal savior. He provides divine satisfaction, "I shall not want." "He leadeth me in the path of righteousness" will give me divine direction. My heart is restored.

Pondering Thoughts
Reflect on the text

He leads through the Holy Spirit, His Word, and the counsel and the teaching of other believers. God leads me into the right path. Divine determination is His purpose; all roads lead to Christ. God is making us in His own image. "Thou art with me" is confident thinking. No matter the valley, suffering, the rod and staff will give determination and reinforcement.

Practical Application
Respond to the text

"Surely goodness and mercy shall follow me all the days of my life," this is divine association. God here speaks of his never-failing ability. Mercy is steadfast loyalty. God never fails nor forsakes us. I am in his residence now in the earthly kingdom and eternal kingdom to come. I have accepted his counsel.

Rule

PSALM 24:1

Primary text
Repeat the text

"The earth is the Lord's, and the fulness thereof; the world and they that dwell within."

Personal Response
Remember the text

The Lord is seen here claiming what is his by right of creation. He is my redeemer and ruler. "Lift up your eyes on high, and behold who hath created these things . . . he is strong in power; not one faileth." (Isaiah 40:26). "Great is the Lord, and greatly to be praised; and his greatness is unsearchable." (Psalm 145:3-4). I have an infinite being that rules my life.

Pondering Thoughts
Reflect on the text

God is my redeemer and ruler. "Thus saith the LORD, the heaven is my throne, and the earth is my footstool . . ." (Isaiah 66:1-2). "For with God nothing shall be impossible." (Luke 1:37). "Am I a God at hand, saith the LORD, and not a God far off?" (Jeremiah 23:23-24). His claims provide my resource to live out His rules.

Practical Application
Respond to the text

God is my redeemer and ruler. "The heavens declare the glory of God; and the firmament sheweth his handiwork." (Psalm 19:1). "Behold, I am the LORD, the God of all flesh. Is there anything too hard for me?" (Jeremiah 32:27). "And God said, let there be light; and there was light." (Genesis 1:3).

My creator God has become my substitute on the cross and justifies. He has provided the rules in his sovereignty for me to obey to be successful in my life. He deserves glory and praise.

I am secure in Him. I live with confidence. I find my rest on His word. His grace provides steadfastness. I worship the one and only true God. I receive blessing because of His presence with me.

Teach

PSALM 25:4

Primary Text
Repeat the text

"Show me thy ways, O Lord, teach me thy paths."

Personal Response
Remember on the text

Chapters 25-39 are full of spiritual food for suffering souls. It can be successful through exercising Biblical truth during trouble and distress. Comfort will be accomplished. They are built on trust: "He trusted in the LORD." The Christian is indwelt by the Supreme Teacher, and given understanding.

Pondering Thoughts
Reflect on the text

This is the spiritual food: "Examine me, O LORD" (Psalm 26:2). "The just shall live by faith" (Hebrews 10:38). "He that doeth the will of God abideth forever" (1 John 2:17).

This is the spiritual food: "Lead me in a plain path" (Psalm 27:1). "A man's heart plans his way, but the LORD directeth his steps" (Proverbs 16:9). "For God hath not given us the spirit of fear but of power, and of love and of a sound mind" (2 Timothy 1:7).

This is the spiritual food: "The LORD will give strength unto his people. The LORD will bless his people with peace" (Psalm 29:11). "Be of good courage and he shall strengthen your heart, all ye that hope in the LORD" (Psalm 31:24).

Practical Application

Respond to the text

This is the spiritual food: "Have mercy on me, O LORD, be thou my helper" (Psalm 30:10). "Fear not; I am the first and the last; behold, I am forevermore" (Revelation 1:17-18. "My help cometh from the LORD, which made heaven and earth. He will not suffer thy foot to be moved, he that keepeth thee will not slumber" (Psalm 121:2-3).

"My God shall supply all my needs" (Philippians 4:8, 11-13). "The LORD is my keeper" (Psalm 121:5-8). "Rest in the LORD and wait" (Psalm 37:5-7).

Fear

PSALM 33:8

Primary Text
Repeat the text

"Let all the earth fear the Lord, and let all the inhabitants of the earth stand in awe of him."

Personal Response
Remember the text

This is continued from the last devotional. Exercise the Biblical truth into everyday life.

This is the spiritual food: "Let all the earth fear the Lord" (Psalm 33:8). "Fear of God is the instruction of wisdom" (Proverbs 15:32-33). "Thy word is a lamp unto my feet and a light unto my path" (Psalm 119:105). "The fear of the Lord is the beginning of wisdom and knowledge and understanding" (Proverbs 9:10).

Pondering Thoughts
Reflect on the text

This is the spiritual food: Take hold of shield and buckler" (Psalm 35:2). "He that dwelleth in the secret place of the Most High shall abide under the shadow of the Almighty" (Psalm 91:1). "I will both lay me down in peace and sleep, for thou, Lord, only makest me dwell in safety" (Psalm 4:8). "How excellent is thy lovingkindness . . . shadow of thy wings" (Psalm 36:7).

Practical Application
Respond to the text

This is the spiritual food: "Forsake me not, O Lord . . . be not far from me" (Psalm 38:21). "O Lord, my salvation" (Psalm 38:22).

This is the spiritual food: "My hope is in thee . . . deliver me from my transgressions" (Psalm 39:7-8). "The Lord is my portion, sayeth my soul" (Lamentations 3:22-24). "Now the God of peace . . . make you perfect in every good work to do his will . . . to whom be glory forever and ever" (Hebrews 13:21).

Substitution
PSALM 40:4

Primary text
Repeat the text

"Blessed is that man that maketh the Lord his trust, and respecteth not the proud, nor such as turn aside to lies."

Personal Response
Remember the text

Man is threefold — "May the God of peace himself sanctify you entirely; and may your spirit and soul and body be preserved complete, without blame at the coming of our Lord Jesus Christ." (1 Thessalonians 5:23).

Man is spirit because he is dependent on God. This is the nucleus of life: the life-principle; the source of life: God-conscious; worshipful part of man; likeness of God. The inbreathing of God was an endless life not subject to death; "and the Lord God formed man of the dust of the ground, and breathed into his nostrils (face) the breath of life and man became a living soul" (Genesis 2:7).

Pondering Thoughts
Reflect on the text

Man is soul because he has the likeness of God and body that links him to earth; and God said, "Let us make man in our image, after our likeness" (Genesis 1:26-27). He has personality, individuality, intellect-mind, understanding; sensibility-emotion; will-decisions.

Man is body because he possesses flesh, bones, nerve, brain, blood — vital organs. And the Lord God formed man of the dust of the ground" (Genesis 2:7). Chemically man has 16 elements of soil represented in his body. Six vital minerals are present in organic form and the remainder being water, carbon and gases. "The first man is from the earth, earthy . . ." (1 Corinthians 15:47).

Practical Application
Respond to the text

"I will praise thee; for I am fearfully and wonderfully made: marvellous are thy works; and that my soul knoweth right well" (Psalm 134:14).

We can live a Christian life because Jesus has regenerated us.

Delight

PSALM 40:8

Primary Text

Repeat the text

"I delight to do thy will, O my God; yea, thy law is within my heart."

Personal Response

Remember the text

This is Jesus Christ's testimony. When on earth, it was His delight to do God's will and His law in His heart. He is the man in the first psalm. His holy walk in preaching righteousness before the cross is here in view. "Thou knowest," He could say to His Father, and the father's voice spoke over His blessed Son declaring that His delight was equally in Him. He witnessed a good confession. The mighty power of God raised him up and gave Him the highest place in glory, where he is now the everlasting witness that the work is done (Isaiah 10:5-10).

Pondering Thoughts
Reflect on the text

In Jesus Christ's testimony, we see deep suffering — patience in waiting and deliverance. A song of praise is given by the Spirit of God. I personally stand behind Psalm 1. "I delight to do thy will" (Psalm 40:8). I am grateful to God for the privilege to study God's law through my delight and pleasure to do so. The study started in my childhood. I have travelled through correspondence, extension, residence, and it was all motivated through love of the person behind the scripture and His very word.

Practical Application
Respond to the text

"Thy law is within my heart." In all my studies, every study has had these foundations through the Bible. My heart has been filled. All the experience has laid the foundation for teacher certification, ordination to ministry and doctorate in religion. My heart delights in God's word.

Blessed
PSALM 41:1

Primary Text
Repeat the text

"Blessed is he that considereth the poor: the Lord will deliver him in time of trouble."

Personal Response
Remember the text

This psalm starts with the word "blessed" and ends with "blessed." It tells us about Jesus' death, suffering and resurrection. The word "poor" refers to being <u>miserable</u>. He paid our penalty for disobedience on the cross. The word "gracious refers to the fact that he was victorious and delivered us. The word blessed refers to the fact that he completed his responsibility and justified us.

My personal response to the word "poor" is that I am a sinner. I have to do something about the sin problem. I am guilty before God. I have to decide to believe God's plan to get into the right relationship. Forgiveness is given when I believe in Jesus' death (my substitution) on the cross has paid the price. Justification by faith in Jesus Christ takes place. (Romans 3:23).

Pondering Thoughts
Reflect on the text

We are involved in a situation from which there was no escape; sin had man it its power and there was no hope. Jesus came into the situation and he brought with him something that broke the old deadlock. His love enabled man to be rescued.

Practical Application
Respond to the text

To confess Jesus Christ through faith, we must accept Him supreme in our own life. Implicit obedience and worship takes place. We must believe that he is risen from the dead. We must believe that Jesus lives and we can know him. We must believe in our own hearts. Christianity is belief plus confession (Romans 10:9-10).

Panteth
PSALM 42:1-2

Primary Text
Repeat the text

"As the hart panteth after the water brooks, so panteth my soul after thee, O God. My soul thirsteth for God, for the living God."

Personal Response
Remember the text

God's desire is for the believer to live with an intense longing for him. I need to be thirsty for God. In my youth, I desired to follow Matthew 6:33, "Seek first the kingdom." The passion has caused my soul to thirst for God (Psalm 42:1-2). As a Christian, I have learned to live with God's promises activated in my life. Faith is a decision to accept, read and interpret God's word in the correct way.

Pondering Thoughts
Reflect on the text

As I seek, I will produce righteousness. It is living out the Christ-like life. It is described in Jesus' own words in Matthew 5:3. He says be humble (attitude toward ourselves), be repentive (attitude toward sin), be pure (attitude toward the best) and be obedient (attitude toward the Holy Spirit). To "seek his kingdom and righteousness" involves his divine presence. It will take desire, discipline, determination and devotion. This will involve God's divine presence, his divine transformation and his divine will.

Practical Application
Respond to the text

The Holy Spirit releases power from inside the spirit. Choose to allow Jesus Christ to dominate life.

As I panteth over God's word, it will cause praise.

Hope
PSALM 43:5

Primary Text
Repeat the text

"Hope in God."

Personal Response
Remember the text

This psalm is closely connected with the preceding one. The Lord Jesus Christ is both, the light and the truth. Jesus Christ is my Lord and Savior. He has been my substitute on the cross. He is my hope. Hope is my expectation that Jesus Christ will be my enablement, strength, leader and joy.

Pondering Thoughts
Reflect on the text

I am encouraged in the Lord's hope provided for me, his child. "It is of the Lord's mercies that we are not consumed, because his compassions fail not. They are new every morning; great is thy faithfulness. The Lord is my portion, saith my soul; therefore I will hope in him." (Lamentations 3:22-24). I experience his compassion. I experience his faithfulness. I experience his hope.

Practical Application
Respond to the text

I enjoy his presence. I am justified by faith. Peace is guarding my life. I experience his hope. (Romans 5:1-5). "Now the God of hope fill you with all joy and peace in believing, that ye may abound in hope, through the power of the Holy Ghost." (Romans 15:13). "My soul, wait thou only upon God; for my expectation is from him." (Psalm 62:5-7).

King
PSALM 44:4

Primary Text
Repeat the text

"Thou art my King, O God..."

Personal Response
Remember the text

In Psalm 44, I was reminded of Moses and Joshua's history. The language of faith and testing took place. Our greatest trouble will become victorious through the King. Jesus Christ is the King of Kings. This is a prophetic hymn.

Pondering Thoughts
Reflect on the text

The word *king* in Hebrew means supreme ruler. He is our judge and justice. He is the absolute master. He has all power to rule. Jesus becomes our king as we accept, believe and confess his name.

Practical Application
Respond to the text

Jesus' kingdom resides in the hearts of his people. The spiritual kingdom requires internal repentance, not just external submission. It provides deliverance from sin rather than the political deliverance. "Behold, the kingdom of God is within you." (Luke 17:21).

Power
PSALM 45:2

Primary text
Repeat the text

". . . Grace is poured into thy lips; therefore God hath blessed thee forever."

Personal Response
Remember the text

The verse speaks of our union with Jesus Christ. It is a heavenly wedding song rejoicing in our relationship with Jesus Christ. I love this text because it written to a musician and based upon our union. My life started and ended with music in teaching, conducting and mentoring. What does it mean to be in Christ and what does it mean Christ in you? The believer is in Christ and Christ is in the believer. He is our position, possession, safekeeper and association. Christ is in the believer given life, character and dynamic for conduct.

Pondering Thoughts
Reflect on the text

God's grace provides "Ye in me and I in you." (John 14:2). Being in Christ is a position which can have no corresponding experience. The presence of 'Christ in you' is the imperishable hope of glory.

My faith in Christ makes me complete in Him.

"I in you" (my acceptance by faith) and "you in me (John 17:20-23) are my acceptance of the indwelling Spirit.

Practical Application
Respond to the text

A divine life depends upon abiding in Christ. "If ye keep my commandments, ye shall abide in my love . . ." (John 15:10). Divine life is Christ indwelling the believer by His Spirit. This is all dependent on faith which receives the saving grace of God. Grace is a superhuman rule of life which grows out of acceptance with God and which is first wrought in the heart and then achieved by the enabling power of the Spirit. Power here means the result of proclaiming God's word.

Refuge
PSALM 46:1

Primary text
Repeat the text

"God is our refuge and strength, a very present help in trouble."

Personal Response
Remember the text

This psalm launches a trilogy (46, 47, 48), songs of triumph. There is no threat, God is present with us. The forces of nature and nations are not fearful. We are stable with God's presence. Those powerful words need to sink into our heads and hearts. "The Lord of hosts is with us." (v. 7). "God is in the midst of her, she shall not be moved." (v. 5). Refuge refers to the fact that God is our helper. He keeps us safe. He takes care of our needs.

Pondering Thoughts
Reflect on the text

God protects us. He is our stronghold (Numbers 14:9). "The God of Jacob is our refuge." (v. 7). He is our fortress. He is dependable. Refuge refers to the fact that God is our strength.

Practical Application
Respond to the text

"The Lord of hosts is with us." — He is our refuge. Holiness will be necessary. "God is with you, be ye holy." (Deuteronomy 23:14). The priority is walking upright. Refuge refers to the fact that God requires holiness. God's presence provides His help, His strength, His holiness. Our refuge is in Him during times of trouble.

Proclamation
PSALM 47:9

Primary text
Repeat the text

"God is greatly exalted."

Personal Response
Remember the text

God is my protection and shield. In Psalm 46, the coming of the king in judgement is celebrated. Now, he is king over all the earth and is praised and worshipped. He will descend and ascend at stated times to display His visible glory. I am looking for ways to exalt him. I will proclaim His name through His power. His power will provide the way, grace to proclaim and exalt Him.

Pondering Thoughts
Reflect on the text

Righteous character will exalt God's name. Christian character flows from within. Our attitudes toward ourselves (Matthew 5:3). To be poor in spirit means to be humble, to have a correct estimate of one's self (Romans 12:3). It is not self-praise or self-assertion. It is honesty with ourselves. We know ourselves, accept ourselves. Our attitude toward sin (Matthew 5:4-6), we see sin the way God sees it. We seek to treat it the way God does. We should submit it to God (Luke 18:9-14, Philippians 3:1-14). It is having power under control.

Practical Application
Respond to the text

Our attitude toward the Lord (Matthew 5:7-9): We experience mercy when we trust in Christ (Ephesians 2:4-7). He gives us a clean heart (Acts 15:9). He gives us peace within (Romans 5:1). We become peacemakers in a troubled world and channels for God's mercy, purity and peace.

Our attitude toward the world (Matthew 5:10-16): We must expect to be persecuted if we are living as God wants us to live. Jesus Christ's beatitudes are my characteristics to exalt God Almighty. As I proclaim God's Word it will cause power.

Guidance
PSALM 48:14, PSALM 49:3

Primary Text
Repeat the text

" . . . God will be our guide even unto death."

Personal Response
Repeat the text

In chapter 48, we read about our guide and in chapter 49, we discern His perspective. We can live with a future that is secure. He has provided direction and strength. We need to practice trust and obey Him. Our destiny is determined by God. He is our delight and counselor. (Psalm 119:24).

Pondering Thoughts
Reflect on the text

In the text, I have found words that describe my guide:

My guide is great — supernatural.
My guide is holy — dedicated.
My guide is loving — caring.
My guide is wise — makes good judgments.
My guide is understanding — clear in thought.

Practical Application
Respond to the text

In the text, I have found words that show his provision for me:

My guide provides refuge — safety in danger.
My guide provides righteousness — upright behavior.
My guide provides hearing — knows my thoughts.
My guide provides wisdom — gives good judgement.
My guide provides stability — be fused with His strength.

"My mouth shall speak of wisdom and the meditations of my heart shall be of understanding." Psalm 49:3.

Judge
PSALM 50:1-6

Primary text
Repeat the text

"The Mighty One, God, the Lord, speaks and summons the earth from the rising of the sun to the place where it sets. The heavens proclaim his righteousness, for God Himself is judge." (NIV)

Personal Response
Remember the text

The Supreme Judge wants worship in spirit and truth. "The hour cometh, and now is, when the true worshipers will worship the Father in spirit and in truth; for the Father seeketh such to worship him. God is a spirit and they that worship him must worship him in spirit and in truth." (John 4:23-24). "The Mighty One wants fear, reverence, honor and humility.

Pondering Thoughts
Reflect on the text

The Supreme Judge doesn't want externalism and hypocrisy. Ritualism and rebellion are condemned. God's desire is to expose these sins and give them opportunity to repent and return to the Lord. Outwardly they give daily sacrifices but inwardly they lacked love and fellowship.

Practical Application
Respond to the text

The description of the true worshipper comes from the heart. Combine these characteristics:

Gratitude — obedience — prayer — desire — confidence — honor.

Now, we can glorify God in our hearts with joy in worship.

Sin

PSALM 51:10

Primary Text
Repeat the text

"Create in me a pure heart, O God, and renew a steadfast spirit within me."

Personal Response
Remember the text

As I look at "pure in heart," I think of the opposite. Impurity, unclean, sin, disobedience, iniquity and satanic. We sin because of choice and by nature (I John 1:8, Psalm 51:5). If we want a pure heart do what Psalm 51 says: Cleanse me (vs 1-7), restore me (vs 8-12) and use me (vs 13-19).

Pondering Thoughts
Reflect on the text

I like "create in me a pure heart." Every day, I have the opposite. Impurity — unclean heart (Psalm 41:6), sin — disobedience (Romans 3:23), iniquity —

satanic (Isaiah 53:6). Remember to keep the commandments (Psalm 119:176). Remember the Redeemer (Titus 2:14).

Practical Application
Respond to the text

I like "create in me a pure heart." We must be filled with the Spirit (Ephesians 5:18). It is a daily process of breathing out sin through confession and breathing in the filling of the Holy Spirit.

Put these thoughts into action:

1. Self-examination (Acts 20:28, I Corinthians 11:28).
2. Confess all known sins (I John 1:9).
3. Submit to God (Romans 6:11-13).
4. Ask for filling (Luke 11:13).
5. Be thankful (1 Thessalonians 5:18).

We are born in sin but we don't have to stay that way (John 14:6).

Mercy
PSALM 52:8

Primary text
Repeat the text

" . . . I trust in the mercy of God for ever and ever."

Personal Response
Remember the text

Psalm 52 contains a great prophetic picture of the coming Antichrist, the man of sin, as he domineers over Israel during the end of the age. He will institute the great tribulation of which Daniel speaks (Daniel 12:1), and which our Lord mentions in His prophetic discourse (Matthew 24). The godly will suffer but they will be gloriously delivered by the coming of the King. "I trust in the mercy of God for ever and ever." In previous chapters, I have thought about the wicked one. The word "mercy" rings loudly in my present condition and others I visit.

Pondering Thoughts
Reflect on the text

"Mercy" in Hebrew means kindness and in Greek means compassion. It is a form of love determined by the state or condition of its objects. It is a ministry of relief. "Blessed are the merciful for they shall obtain mercy" (Matthew 5:7).

The word "blessed" implies our inner satisfaction and sufficiency that did not depend on outward circumstances for happiness. It is our attitude. We experience God's mercy when we trust Christ (Ephesians 2:4-7). He gives us a clean heart (Acts 15:9) and peace within (Romans 5:1). We have become peacemakers in a troubled world and channels for God's mercy, purity and peace.

Practical Application
Respond to the text

Mercy is kindness. It is showing zeal toward good sense. It is given favor and benefits (Genesis 21:33, 2 Samuel 10:2). It practices compassion for the afflicted (Job 6:14). Mercy, kindness, compassion is the formula to do. Goodness is the key (2 Corinthians 6:6, Ephesians 2:7, Colossians 3:12). Peace has become the result of glorifying God.

Deceived
PSALM 53:1

Primary text
Repeat the text

"The fool hath said in his heart, there is no God."

Personal Response
Remember the text

Let's look at three major words. "The fool" in the Bible is often an ethical concept and goes beyond a lack of intelligence. He is one who lacks the wisdom which comes with the knowledge of God. In the Old testament, his pride is wise in his own eyes and acts contrary to the will of God. He denies God's existence. (Psalm 14:1).

In the New Testament, the fool is one who refuses to recognize the truth of God as communicated through the life and resurrection of Jesus Christ (Luke 24:25, 1 Corinthians 15:36).

Pondering Thoughts
Reflect on the text

The second word is "heart." In Hebrew we find it 854 times Its central meaning is "core." It is a physical organ in the body. In relationship to the spirit it is emotion, intellectual and mind. It is the seat of the will. The deepest meaning is that the heart will determine the response to God's revelation to man. The fool cannot see it but the believer in Christ can understand it.

Practical Application
Respond to the text

The third word is "no." These words draw a picture of the people that say "there is no God."

Creeping corruption into the church through deception.

Scoffing language will be heard through mocking.

Blasphemy directed toward the Biblical authority.

Lawlessness is the liberal mindset.

Heretic unbelief destroying the word of God and the church.

Helper
PSALM 54:4

Primary text
Repeat the text

"God is my helper; the Lord is with them that uphold my soul."

Personal Response
Repeat the text

Psalms 52-55 give a prophetic picture of the coming great tribulation. We read about the story of the man of sin. We see the increase of atheism. God is denied. The Bible is not the trustworthy, infallible revelation of God. Evolution is adopted by the world. We read, "In the beginning, God . . ." Genesis is considered a myth. We see deep distress. We see suffering. We will see the cry of faith.

Pondering Thoughts
Reflect on the text

"God is my helper" (v. 4). We have been given a gift of faith in salvation. My spiritual participation in fellowship will enable me in faith. Faith finds its basis in God and His character. We can trust God's word because He is trustworthy. The infinite perfection of God stands behind what he says. The Holy Scripture is divinely inspired (2 Timothy 3:16, 17,). Jesus Christ has confirmed the word of God. Check John 12:48, John 15:7, John 8:31-32, Matthew 12:2-3, Matthew 4:2-4.

Practical Application
Respond to the text

The attribute of faith is a decision, choice, response by way of the will. Faith is taking God at his word (Hebrews 11:4-8). Faith is a decision based on God's Word. Biblical application is to choose. Make up your mind to choose. Do we find our delight and satisfaction in Him and His will? Are we motivated by His promises?

"Without faith it is impossible to please Him (Hebrews 11:6). We must decide, choose and follow God's will.

Communication
PSALM 55:17

Primary Text
Repeat the text

"Evening, morning, and at noon, will I pray and he shall hear my voice."

Personal Response
Remember the text

The verse gives us a challenge to pray all day long. We can look up to God and trust Him (v. 16-19, 22-23). We will have difficult times. We can go through bad circumstances (vs 9-15, 20, 21). Our feelings can cause issues (vs 1-5). We can look at a safe refuge (vs 6-8). Let's learn to pray — communicating to God.

Pondering Thoughts
Reflect on the text

<u>Prayer involves consuming passion</u>. God's glory is my concern. "I have glorified thee upon the earth" (John 17:4). Jesus is my model. He secured God's glory by completing the task entrusted to him. I have deep passion as I talk to my heavenly Father, my God. "I always do the things that are pleasing to him" (John 8:29). This is my desire. I adore "Our Heavenly Father."

Prayer involves secret dialogue. "Pray to your Father who is in secret" (Matthew 6:6). Jesus is my model, shut in with God, shut out from all else. Rewards will be provided. "Thy Father which seeth in secret shall reward thee" (Matthew 6:6). Private time with God is necessary. Have a habit in meeting alone with him.

Prayer involves a place of solitude. Jesus is our model. He has spent whole nights in prayer (Luke 6:12). He has prayed undisturbed (Matthew 14:13,23; Mark 6:46; Luke 5:16; John 18:2). Prayer will prevail with concentration in His presence.

Practical Application
Respond to the text

Practice God's word in prayer.
Have faith (Mark 1:22),
Pray in Jesus' name (John 14:14).

Faith

PSALM 56:3

Primary Text

Repeat the text

"I will put my trust and faith in you."

Personal Response

Remember the text

In Psalm 56 we read about despair and doubt. David prayed for deliverance from death (vs 1-4), from stumbling (vs 5-11) and the ability to praise (vs 12-13). Trust and faith are common with the word confidence. Read these verses and act upon them. Exhortation regarding faith:

Live by faith — Romans 1:7
Walk by faith — Romans 4:12
Pray by faith — Matthew 21:22
Resist evil by faith — Ephesians 6:16

Pondering Thoughts
Reflect on the text

Receive by faith these verses and put them into action. Practice regarding faith:

Purity of heart — Acts 15:9
Forgiveness, sanctification — Acts 26:18
Comfort of fellowship — Romans 1:12

Practical Application
Respond to the text

The believer is one who has received the Lord Jesus Christ by believing on Him (John 1:12) and now has the ability to live by faith (2 Corinthians 5:7, Galatians 2:20, Hebrews 11). Faith is personal and based on the character of the one we believe (Romans 4:17-21). Faith and trust are not based on emotion or circumstances (vs 18-19).

Accept the power of God as true and interpret on the basis of the attributes of God. (vs 20-21).

Access to God — Romans 5:2
Jesus' presence — Ephesians 3:17

Steadfast

PSALM 57:7

Primary Text

Repeat the text

"My heart is steadfast, O God, my heart is steadfast. I will sing and make music."

Personal Response

Remember the text

This psalm covers one day in David's life as a fugitive, verse 4 records his lying down and verse 8 his waking up. "I am in the midst of lions" (v. 4). "Awake, my soul" (v. 8). This reminded me of the comforter, my helper — the Holy Spirit. "Great is your love . . . Be exalted, O God" (vs 10-11).

The Holy Spirit is a person. He is a real person and understands me. In John 16:13-14, proves Him beyond all doubt, that the Comforter is a real person. Look up the text in John and underline each word that provides proof. They are (1) He comes, (2) He guides, (3) He hears, (4) He speaks, (5) He glorifies, (6) He receives, (7) He shows. He is not only power and influence, but a person.

Pondering Thoughts
Reflect on the text

There are seven principal words used in connection with the presence and work of the Holy Spirit:

Born — John 3:5,6
Indwelt — 2 Timothy 1:4, Romans 8:11
Sealed — 2 Timothy 1:22, Ephesians 1:13, 4:30
Earnest — 2 Corinthians 1:22, Ephesians 1:14
Anointed — 2 Corinthians 1:21, 1 John 2:27
Filled — Luke 1:15, 41,67; Acts 4:8, 4:17; Ephesians 5:18
Baptize — Matthew 3:11; Acts 1:5; 1 Corinthians 12:13

Each word has its own significance.

Practical Application
Respond to the text

We have read about the Holy Spirit's person, principles, and now partakers. "Your body is the temple of the Holy Spirit that is in you" (1 Corinthians 6:19).

Are we indwelt with God's gracious work (Galatians 5:22,23): Love, joy, peace, patience, kindness, goodness, faithfulness, gentleness and self-control. "Live by the Spirit, let us keep in step with the Spirit" (Galatians 5:25).

Reward
PSALM 58:11

Primary Text
Repeat the text

"There is a reward for the righteous . . ."

Personal Response
Remember the text

God will judge the lawless (v. 1-5). God's vengeance will be seen (Deuteronomy 32:35, Hebrews 10:13, Romans 18:19). A judgement day is coming (Psalm 118:12, 2 Samuel 23:6). There is also a day of reward for the righteous. We have responsibility to identify with Christ and to demonstrate His character, not sinful patterns (Ephesians 4:20-24). We must delight in His will (Psalm 40:8), and submit our will to God (James 4:7). We need to develop a renewed mind (Romans 12:2), and and set our desires on things above (Colossians 3:1). With this direction, wisdom, understanding and discretion will guard us from evil (Proverbs 3:10-12) and lead us to rewards unconditional. Surrender is the key.

Pondering Thoughts
Reflect on the text

"There is a reward for the righteous" (v. 11). It involves an act of surrender, which is yieldedness. We have to be conscious of God's nearness. We have to acknowledge our sin (Romans 12:1-2). Surrender involves repentance. We have to be conscious of our inadequacy. We have to acknowledge His ownership (John 15:4). Surrender involves dependence. It starts with simple trust. It continues with committing every matter to Him. It will go forever. "The Lord is my shepherd" (Psalm 23:1).

Practical Application
Respond to the text

"There is a reward for the righteous." I am working on these objectives:

Faithful servant — 1 Corinthians 3:14
Seeking righteousness — 1 Corinthians 9:25
Sharing faith — 1 Thessalonians 2:19
Sustain trials — 1 Corinthians 10:13

"If any man's work abides, he will receive a reward" (1 Corinthians 3:14).

Defend
PSALM 59:1

Primary Text
Repeat the text

"Deliver me from mine enemies, O my God; defend me from them that rise up against me."

Personal Response
Remember the text

The focus of the psalm is on God — the Deliverer (vs 1-9) and the Judge (vs 10-17). The Lord is our fortress. Action on our part in faith has to take place. We don't have to be afraid. The Lord will fight for us (v. 10). He will prepare the way for victory. He is our defense. God's power is received through the development of His thoughts saturating our thoughts (1 Corinthians 2:11, 12). The more I think upon God's word, the more I will think like him. His view of things will become my views. His attitudes will become mine. My defense is the vastness of an infinite God.

Pondering Thoughts
Reflect on the text

The human brain is the single most complex apparatus of all God's vast creative genius. The heart is smaller than my brain no less impressive. The brain is the center of my thinking, and the heart representing affection, emotion and personality. I have to love the Lord with my heart (Mark 12:30) and to keep my heart with all diligence for out of is springs the issues of life (Proverbs 4:23). The heart and brain work together to defend me with God's perspective.

Practical Application
Respond to the text

God's infinity and man's heart can be nourished through observation, interpretation and application. The supernatural power of God can be infused in me through the Holy Spirit. Accepting God's authority, then applying it and studying it will make me think like God. The Bible alone realistically and sufficiently meet man's deepest problems. It is my defense (2 Timothy 3:16, 17; Psalm 119:1). Let the word of God inspire and bless your heart. It takes discipline.

Holy

PSALM 60:6
Part One

Primary text
Repeat the text

"God hath spoken in his holiness. I will rejoice."

Personal Response
Remember the text

This chapter speaks of the scattered Israel. It speaks of the glorious ways of David. We see a national lamentation (v. 1-3). We see the pain of disaster (v. 5). Trust will win the battle. God hath spoken in His holiness. I see God's holiness in the banner (v. 4).

Pondering Thoughts
Reflect on the text

We will have victory if we follow God's holiness. This characteristic sets him apart from his creation; majesty links holiness to sovereignty. His will is linked with holiness. It is supreme and unique. Wrath is linked with holiness. He takes himself seriously and will judge anyone against him. Righteousness is linked to holiness; when God is right, he is right. God stands absolutely as Lord of his creation. He rejects any attacks on his rights.

Practical Application
Respond to the text

God says, "You shall be holy, for I am holy" (1 Peter 1:15-16). It does not say 'Be holy *as* I am holy.' The believer's holiness comes through righteousness. Righteousness comes through transformation in belief. Belief comes through faith. Holiness is our banner for life.

Holy

PSALM 60:6, 1 PETER 1:15-16

Part Two

Primary Text

Repeat the text

"God hath spoken in his holiness; I will rejoice."
"You shall be holy, for I am holy."

Personal Application

Remember the text

The glory of Christianity is its message that the holy God has done something. He has made for us a way into his presence through the Lord Jesus Christ. As a result, the unholy becomes holy and is enabled to dwell within him. The perfect Lamb of God is our sacrifice. We must learn to hate sin. We have to come to God through faith in Jesus Christ. We will learn to love righteousness. We must look to the day when God will be fully known in his holiness.

Pondering Thoughts
Reflect on the text

In Psalm 60, we are reminded of God's holiness. In Psalms 61-69, we discover the way to holiness. <u>Suffering</u> teaches that *constant trust* leads to holiness. <u>Seeking</u> teaches that *right thinking* leads to holiness. <u>Supplication</u> teaches that *relationship* leads to holiness. <u>Submission</u> teaches that *willful attitude* leads to holiness. <u>Spiritual songs</u> teaches that *intimacy* leads to holiness.

Practical Application
Respond to the text

Psalms are about God and his relationship to his creation, the nations of the world, Israel and his believing people. He is seen as a powerful God as well as a tender-hearted Father, a God who keeps his promises and lovingly cares for his people. We learn to accept trials and turn them into triumphs. It shows us how to repent and receive God's gracious forgiveness.

Suffering

PSALM 61:7, PSALM 62:5

Primary Text

Repeat the text

"Wait thou only upon God; for my expectation is from him."

Personal Response

Remember the text

I'm not alone, a lot of people suffer. I wish it would come to an end . . . You know what I mean . . . an instant cure. I realize God has permitted suffering. He knew that the plan He chose, even though it allowed for sin and suffering, ultimately would bring about the greatest good and glory. Our suffering is directly related to the curse that came upon the earth as the result of sin. With sin came corruption, suffering and death. This is not to say that every occurrence of suffering in our lives is direct punishment for our personal sins. The sooner we accept the reality that we are living in a fallen world with its suffering, the sooner we will be able to get on with living effectively.

Pondering Thoughts
Reflect on the text

It has helped me to know the facts. Fear is dreadful but fear in God is hopeful. "The Lord is my light and my salvation . . . whom shall I fear? (Psalm 27:11). My anxiety, tension and uneasiness lessens when I think right. I have had to identify the problem clearly without adding to it . . . discussing with reliable sources. I have had to commit it to the Lord through being more aware of Him than the sickness. I have had to release it to Him. He is quite able to handle it and finally, I have had to stand firm and not retreat in my decision. His Word must be implanted in my mind and heart (Hebrews 8:10). I am able to think right when Jesus Christ is personalized in my life.

Practical Application
Respond to the text

It has helped me to know that the Holy Spirit makes intercession for me as well as Jesus Christ. When I cannot read Scripture, pray, or even accept the comfort of others, I am assured that I'm not left to my own resources. He keeps on helping me. He knows my needs, my very mind and heart. He knows the end from the beginning. He knows what is necessary. He intercedes to enable me to meet each crisis.

Seek

PSALM 63:1, PSALM 64:10

Primary Text
Repeat the text

"O God, thou art my God, early will I seek thee."

Personal Response
Remember the text

Seeking teaches that right thinking leads to holiness. To think right means that I have experienced spiritual insight through Biblical understanding. When I put Jesus' words into action, I will find contentment, rest and holiness. I am learning to be helpless (poor in spirit). This is not financial security. Helplessness is total trust. I am learning to be repentive (mournful). Mourning refers to a sincere sorrow for sin. I understand sin as God does. I don't cover up sin. I learn to be in submission. Repentance means a change of mind. I am learning to surrender (meek). Meekness refers to living for the glory of God. There is no room for self-will. I have to learn to accept God's dealings with me without resistance or disputes.

Pondering Thoughts
Reflect on the text

I am learning to crave (hunger). Contentment can only be experienced through craving after righteousness (holiness). Craving has a driving force behind it. Inner passion is a blessing. Hunger is a passionate drive to please God. I am learning to practice empathy (mercy). Mercy is defined as being compassionate. Sympathy is the ability to share the feelings of another, and this leads to empathy. It is like getting into the skin of others.

Practical Application
Respond to the text

I am learning to be genuine. The pure in heart shall see God. Being authentic, sincere and honest is necessary. I have a single heart. My life is transformed by the grace of God. This leads to holiness. I am learning to be in harmony (peacemaker). I am learning to have peace with God, peace with self, and peace with others.

Righteousness and holiness come from Jesus Christ (Ephesians 4:24).

Supplication

PSALM 65:2, PSALM 66:19

Primary Text
Repeat the text

"O thou that hearest prayer! To thee all flesh shall come."

Personal Response
Remember the text

"Our Father" emphasizes individual and community relationship, not exclusiveness. It is an attitude of tender belonging. It is an intimate connection with "The Mighty God" (Luke 1:49).

The words "who art in heaven" describe a place and an attitude of majesty. Our father is above all. He is sovereign. Our resources are from heaven. They are supernatural and unlimited. Confidence, awe, adoration and reverence become a part of our daily life when we think of heaven and God's presence.

These special words, "hallowed be Thy name," open up a whole dimension of respect, reverence, awe, appreciation, honor, glory, adoration and worship. It means that God is holy. To hallow God's name means to hold his matchless being in reverence so that we will believe what he says and obey him.

Pondering Thoughts
Reflect on the text

"Thy kingdom come" are simple words but incredible in their meaning. "Thy" emphasizes God's kingdom, not human kingdom. "Kingdom" refers to Christ reigning in our hearts and living in a conscious awareness of His presence. It's living with the daily promise of Matthew 6:33, "Seek ye first the kingdom of God and His righteousness, and all these things will be added unto you." Jesus reigns and is sovereign.

Practical Application
Respond to the text

"God forgive my sin in Jesus' name . . . freely I must learn to forgive others." God pardons my sin (Micah 7:18-19). It was laid on Christ (Isaiah 53:6) and it is blotted out (Isaiah 43:25) when I make confession with the mouth and believe in my heart (Romans 10:9-10). Forgiving others and ourselves involves daily confession (1 John 1:9). Forgiveness is an act of the will . . . in which a decision is made to cancel, release or let go of the debt and a process begins which may result in restitution or rekindled feelings. It starts with God's forgiveness and flows through us to others.

Submission

PSALM 66:19, PSALMS 68, 69

Primary Text
Repeat the text

"God has surely listened and heard my voice . . ."

Personal Response
Remember the text

I would like to be a righteous man and have great power and wonderful results in my prayer life. Maybe you do as well! As I was praying about this and thinking with my Bible in hand, the model prayer came to mind, especially one phrase, "thy will be done." Real praying is saying "thy will be done" to God and mean it. It is not coaxing, pestering, or battering God to answer our prayers. Praying is communicating to our heavenly Father.

Pondering Thoughts
Reflect on the text

The word "*our*" refers to the fact that God is not any man's exclusive possession. He belongs to all of us if we are his disciples. This scripture is instruction to Jesus' followers. We matter to God. He is might, majesty and power, but still approachable to us. My foundation in communication to God is salvation (1 Corinthians 15:1-6). "Our" is personal.

The word "*Father*" settles our relationship. We belong to God. He cares and is merciful.

The words "*who is in heaven.*" These words emphasize reverence, awe, adoration, wonder. When we say these words, we speak of love and power. We can be frustrated or defeated but he is undefeatable.

The words "*hallowed be thy name*" . . . the meaning is clear to let God's name be given a position that is absolutely unique. It is different and separate. It reminds us of his character and nature.

Practical Application
Respond to the text

The words "*give us today bread*" . . . Christianity aims at the body, mind and spirit. God is interested in our whole being, a simple petition to take care of our needs for every day.

The words "*forgive us our debts*" . . . is sin missing the mark, stepping across from right to wrong, slipping, willingly breaking the law, failure in duty. If we confess we will be cleansed and given freedom.

Song

PSALM 69:30

Primary Text
Repeat the text

"I will praise the name of God with a song, and will magnify him with thanksgiving."

Personal Response
Remember the text

Spiritual songs lead to holiness. In my late teens, my dad and I wrote a song based on Ephesians 5:18 ("Be filled with the Spirit"). In heaven, I will be complete in holiness. Our song "A Touch of Heaven on Earth" leads the way:

"Would you like a touch of Heaven — here on earth?
And a love and joy — enduring as the surf.
Peace like a river, even temper as our Giver.
Gentle goodness and a faith that's twice its worth?

Would you like a power unequalled in all the earth?
And a sound mind in sorrow, or in mirth.
Then follow the Master's every command as you walk
    the world hand in hand.
And you'll have your touch of Heaven — here on earth!

Pondering Thoughts
Reflect on the text

Spiritual songs lead to holiness. In my late twenties, my wife Joy and I wrote a song based on Psalm 16:8 ("I have set the Lord always before me"). Faith in God brings inner holiness and gives desire.

My one desire is to be like Thee
Cleanse me with Thy love's pure fire
May every precept Thou hast taught into my daily life be wrought
Lord let me do thy will divine
Let each new dawn bring me more like Thee
Grant me Thy peace and keep me pure in heart and mind
This is my prayer I request.

Practical Application
Respond to the text

Spiritual songs lead to holiness. In my late thirties, my family wrote this song based on Psalm 119:133 ("Order my steps in thy word . . ."). I know guidance will be provided to obtain holiness. The song is simple. Respond to its words . . .

Guide my steps, Lord Jesus, and lead me in your way
I want to be like you each moment of the day
Keep me from all sin and cleanse me within
Let God's Word be my power and strengthen me each hour.

Awesome
PSALM 70:1-5

Primary Text
Repeat the text

"Let God be exalted" (v. 4)

Personal Response
Remember the text

It is always good to look back and recall the goodness of the trouble or trial. Ultimate success depends on faith in the Lord and patience during his providential work. Be enthusiastic about telling what God has done (vs 1-2).

Pondering Thoughts
Reflect on the text

Through God's greatness, we have a rejoicing heart (v. 4). He strengthens and accomplishes His purpose and provides inner peace and power. "In the beginning God created the heavens and the earth" (Genesis 1:1). The Hebrew word for God here is Elohim, a plural word. God lets us know He is plural even as He is the singular. The Father is called God (Galatians 1:1-3, Ephesians 1:2-3). The son is called God (John 20:28). The Holy Spirit is called God (Acts 5:3-4). The plurality of God in creation gives His transcendent essence. He is awesome, supreme, great and exalted.

Practical Application
Respond to the text

Knowing God is the most important study that could occupy our minds. His name tells us the meaning of His greatness. "God said to Moses, 'I am that I am . . . I Am hath sent me unto you'" (Exodus 3:14). The words "I am that I am" mean "I am the one who is." This is an expression of God's being: unchanging, eternal, self-existence. Knowing God is the foundation and motivation for everything else in the Christian life. God wants us to know Him because nothing else matters without Him.

Sovereign
PSALM 71:1-24

Primary Text
Repeat the text

"For you have been my hope, O Sovereign Lord, my confidence since my youth." (v. 5)

Personal Response
Remember the text

As believers, we will have enemies. "Deliver me, O my God, from the hand of the wicked, from the grasp of evil and cruel men" (v. 4). "My enemies speak against me; those who wait to kill me conspire together" (v. 10). "My accusers . . . want to harm me" (v. 13). The Lord is my refuge (v. 1). He is my rock (v. 3).

Pondering Thoughts
Reflect on the text

Don't run away and hide from life but receive the strength needed to face life with its challenges (v. 1-4). In discouragement and worry, look back and count your blessings (v. 5-13). Trust the Lord; he helps in the past, present and future. Hope continually (v. 14). Trust in God, the trials will work for us and not count against us and will lead to glory (2 Corinthians 4:16-18; Romans 5:1-5).

Practical Application
Respond to the text

Look back at trials and blessings. Praise God for His help (v. 22-24). Look up and find confidence. "Your righteousness reaches to the skies, O God, you who have done great things. Who, O God, is like you?" (v. 19). God's sovereignty is working for you and me.

Deeds

PSALM 72:1-20

Primary Text

Repeat the text

"God alone does marvelous deeds." (v. 18)

Personal response

Remember the text

God's kingdom will be a just reign (v. 1-4). God's justice will be faithful. The earth will radiate with God's rule. His justice and compassion will be seen.

God's kingdom will be a universal reign (v. 5-11). It will grow and be famous. It has little limitation.

God's kingdom will be a compassionate reign (v. 12-14). It will help the needy and afflicted. It will rescue the oppressed.

God's kingdom will be a prosperous reign (v. 15-17). It will flourish. It will endure forever. It will be blessed.

God's kingdom will be a glorious reign (v. 19-20).

God's marvelous deeds will be seen. May the whole earth be filled with his glory.

Pondering Thoughts
Reflect on the text

Psalm 72 is a prophetic glimpse of God's kingdom. Jesus Christ will reign as King of righteousness. He will rule as a sovereign King. His kingdom will have no end (Luke 18:32-33). He said his kingdom is at hand (Matthew 4:17). The kingdom is in the midst of us (Luke 17:21). I want to reach God's kingdom. He says (seek first his kingdom" (Matthew 6:33). Spirit and Kingdom requires internal repentance, not just external submission. How, it is a spiritual rule (Like 17:21). Later, it will be established in a literal earthly kingdom (Revelation 20:4-6).

Practical Application
Respond to the text

As I practice the fruit of the Spirit in Galatians 5:22-23, I will manifest His kingdom. His marvelous deeds will be shared.

Guide

PSALM 73:1-28

Primary Text

Repeat the text

"I am always with you; you hold me by my right hand. You guide me with your counsel, and afterward you will take me into glory." (vs 23-24)

Personal Response

Remember the text

Why do the righteous suffer when the ungodly seem to prosper? "Surely God is good to Israel, to those who are pure in heart. But as for me, my feet had almost slipped . . ." (v. 1-2). Hold on to what you know for sure — never doubt in the darkness what God has taught you in the light. His counsel will stand against the enemy. Don't envy the wicked. In struggles just believe, the unbelieving person will not believe. Surrender to God and slipping away will disappear.

Pondering Thoughts
Reflect on the text

Don't serve God for what you get out of it. Serve because He is worthy of it. God is awesome in His sanctuary. Commune with Him and see the things of this world in their right perspective. Don't consider the circumstances around you, but the destiny before you.

Practical Application
Respond to the text

The righteous are guided by God's truth (v.24). Stand for the truth. Don't slip from the truth. Don't struggle with evil. Be firmly grounded in the truth. Psalm 73 deals with a personal crisis of faith. God's hand will keep us in His counsel.

Shine
PSALMS 80-83

Primary Text
Repeat the text

". . . O God, make your face shine upon us . . ." (Psalm 80:3)

Personal Response
Remember the text

I want to encourage you to prayerfully — and carefully — read each verse. Write some notes, highlight the key thoughts, write on the margins. When you have finally wrapped your mind and heart around these truths, don't be silent.

Pondering Thoughts
Reflect on the text

"<u>Restore</u> us, O Lord God Almighty. Make your face shine upon us, that we may be saved." (Psalm 80:19).

"Let your hand <u>rest</u> on the man at your right hand." (Psalm 80: 17).

"In your distress you called and I <u>rescued</u> you." (Psalm 81:7).

"I satisfy you from my rock." (Psalm 81:16).

Practical Application
Respond to the text

"Rescue the weak and needy, deliver them from the hand of the wicked." (Psalm 82:4).

"Rise up, O God, judge the earth, for all the nations are your inheritance." (Psalm 82:8).

"O God, do not keep silent." (Psalm 83:1).

Favorites
PSALMS 84-89

Primary Text
Repeat the text

"How lovely is your dwelling place, O Lord Almighty." (Psalm 84:1)

Personal Response
Remember the text

". . . my heart and my flesh cry out for the living God." (Psalm 84:2)

". . . Blessed are those who dwell in your house; they are ever praising you." (Psalm 84:4)

"Hear my prayer, O Lord God Almighty; listen to me, God of Jacob." (Psalm 84:8)

Pondering Thoughts
Reflect on the text

"Will you not revive us again, that your people may rejoice in you?" (Psalm 85:6)

"Righteousness . . . prepares the way for his steps." (Psalm 85:13)

"You, Lord . . . abound in love to all who call to you." (Psalm 86:5)

"I call to you, for you will answer me." (Psalm 86:7)

Practical Application
Respond to the text

"As they make music they will sing, 'All my fountains are in you.'" (Psalm 87:7)

"May my prayer come before you; turn your ear to my cry." (Psalm 88:2)

"I will sing of the Lord's great love forever; with my mouth I will make your faithfulness known to all generations." (Psalm 89:1)

"Blessed are those who have learned to acclaim you, who walk in the light of your presence, Lord." (Psalm 89:15)

Generations
PSALM 90:1-17

Primary text
Repeat the text

"So teach us to number our days, that we may apply our hearts unto wisdom."

"Lord, thou hast been our dwelling place in all generations."

Personal Response
Remember the text

This meditation is written to remind us of our days on earth and family relations in past generations. Psalms describes every possible kind of human experiences. It is a book of devotion, worship and hope. It is divided into five parts.

Pondering Thoughts

Reflect on the text

"Let God be magnified" through our generations.

Psalms 1-44 contain the book of Genesis. The two names Jehovah and Elohim are found in Psalms and Genesis. We find the foundation of God's revelation.

Psalms 42-72 contain the book of Exodus. It describes the suffering of God's people. Deliverance is provided.

Psalms 73-89 contain the book of Leviticus. God is holy and separate. God is the priority for life.

Psalms 90-106 contain the book of Numbers. It is a wandering nation. It is a history of failure.

Practical Application

Respond to the text.

Psalms 107-150 contain the book of Deuteronomy. Praise is the theme. Psalms begins with "blessed is thy name' and ends with 'praise ye the Lord.' Will our families magnify God?

Abide
PSALM 91:1-16

Primary text
Repeat the text

"He that dwelleth in the secret places of the Most High shall abide under the shadow of the Almighty."

Personal Response
Remember the text

God is my 'dwelling place' (v.1). It speaks about the shortness and preciousness of life. I am safe in his supernatural presence. Review the next few chapters; my refuge (Psalm 91:2), my rock (Psalm 92:15), my ruler (Psalm 93:1), my rest (Psalm 94:13), my rejoicing (Psalm 95:11), my righteousness (Psalm 97:6), my King (Psalm 98:6) and my worship (Psalm 99:9). I am abiding in Christ when I practice each of those thoughts.

Pondering Thoughts
Reflect on the text

We are under the 'shadow of the Almighty' (Psalm 91:1). God is spirit, he exists everywhere at the same time. He is everywhere equally all the time. He is free from limitations. In Him we live and move and exist. God is with you if you sense Him, feel Him or not. We are His temple. Rest in His promise "Don't fear for I am with you" (Isaiah 41:10)

Practical Application
Respond to the text

The "Almighty" lives in me. I am His dwelling place (1 Corinthians 6:19). "In Him we live" (Acts 17:28). We are under God's shadow (Psalm 91:1). "He is at my right hand" (Psalm 16:8). His presence is real.

Serve

PSALM 100:1-5

Primary Text
Repeat the text

"Serve the Lord with gladness. Come before his presence with singing" (Psalm 100:2).

Personal Response
Remember the text

"We are his workmanship, created in Christ Jesus for good works, which God prepared beforehand, that we should walk in them" (Ephesians 2:10). Justification by faith takes place (Ephesians 2:8-10). God appoints works. It is our obligation to do good works. It is our service to glorify God. We are the salt of the earth (Matthew 5:13-16).

Pondering Thoughts
Reflect on the text

"Know ye that the Lord, he is God; it is he that hath made us, and not we ourselves; we are his people and the sheep of his pasture" Psalm 100:3). Our service will be evidence of salvation. Our new creation in Christ is an expression of love seen in our service (1 John 3:14). We should serve others faithfully. A major part of Jesus' ministry was service to others. Be delighted and challenged through Jesus Christ's service in the gospels.

Practical Application
Respond to the text

"Know that the Lord is God (Psalm 100:3). Confidence comes from knowing who is in charge.

"Serve the Lord with gladness (Psalm 100:1-2). Conduct is right in our worship of God.

"Enter his gates with thanksgiving" (Psalm 100:4). Character is joyful over relationship with God.

"His truth endureth to all generations" (Psalm 100:5). Our children for generations will produce future goals.

Blameless
PSALM 101:1-8

Primary Text
Repeat the text

"I will be careful to lead a blameless life. When will you come to me?" (v. 2)

Personal Response
Remember the text

When I serve the Lord I must serve with a blameless life. A life that is centered with confession. Jesus Christ is my example: "Lo, I come to do thy will, O God" (Hebrews 10:7). "I will declare thy name in the midst of the church" (Hebrews 2:12). I will not tolerate sin. The Holy Spirit will be my helper.

Pondering Thoughts
Reflect on the text

The Bible says "Quench not the Spirit" (1 Thessalonians 5:19). I must learn to resist the enemy. Stop saying no to the Holy Spirit. Stop refusing to yield to the word of God. Stop saying no to his guidance. We need to have a constant attitude of yieldedness rather than rebellion. Every day decisions are involved. We have to learn to stop rejecting the Spirit. The Bible says, "Don't grieve the Holy Spirit of God" (Ephesians 4:30). Our fellowship is with a person and the relationship can never be right as long as we continue in unconfessed and unforsaken sin.

Practical Application
Respond to the text

The third condition is, stop walking in the flesh. We need to practice a moment by moment relationship with the Spirit who dwells within us. Dependence on the Spirit is necessary. "Walk in Him" (Colossians 2:6). "Be filled with the Spirit (Ephesians 5:18). Be dominated by the Spirit constantly. This is a moment by moment walk.

To be God's servant: Stop resisting the Spirit. Stop sinning against the Spirit. Stop walking in the flesh.

Cry

PSALM 102:1-28

Primary Text
Repeat the text

"Hear my prayer, O Lord; let my cry for help come to you. Do not hide your face from me when I am in distress. Turn your ear to me when I call, answer me quickly" (vs 1-2).

Personal Response
Remember the text

Learn to pray the word of God. He knows my circumstances. We have to learn to respond to the Lord. We must practice faith that He has given. He will fulfill his promises. We must stand up for the Lord. He will keep to His word. God will assure us of His presence. We may be afflicted. We may cry because of our pain but God will listen and restore us. Keep in mind who made you and who strengthens you.

Pondering Thoughts

Reflect on the text

What does it mean to pray the word of God?

"He reached down from on high and took hold of me; he drew me out of deep waters.: (Psalm 18:16).

"Do not hide your face from me; do not turn your servant away in anger; you have been my helper." (Psalm 27:9).

"Turn your ear to me, come quickly to my rescue . . . you are my rock and my fortress." (Psalm 31:2).

Practical Application

Respond to the text

Practice praying the word of God in action.

John 16:24 "Ask and you will receive."

John 15:17 "The Father will give you whatever you ask."

Magnify
PSALM 103:1-22

Primary text
Repeat the text

"Bless the Lord, O my soul, and all that is within me, bless his holy name — forget not all his benefits." (vs 1-2).

Personal Response
Remember the text

This is a devotional psalm. It is a composition of praise. It is a psalm praising the authority of God's word. We must magnify God with our innermost being.

My sin has been forgiven. I am justified and able to stand before God free.

"God, being rich in mercy, because of His great love with which he loved us, even when we were dead in our transgression, made us alive together with Christ (by grace you have been saved)." (Ephesians 2:4-5).

Pondering Thoughts
Reflect on the text

He provides righteousness and judgement (verse 6). "God is light and in Him there is no darkness at all" (1 John 1:5). We are to live separated lives. God has always judged sin. God's judgement is hell (Matthew 25:14; Hebrews 12:29).

Practical Application
Respond to the text

"There is no creature hidden from His sight, but all things are open and laid bare to the eyes of Him with whom we have to do." (Hebrews 4:13). "In him we live and move and exist." (Acts 17:28).

"Be filled up to all the fulness of God." (Ephesians 3:10-20).

Through these blessed words our prayer should be "I can't, Lord, but You can."

Meditations
PSALM 104:1-35

Primary Text
Repeat the text

"I will sing to the Lord all my life; I will sing praise to my God as long as I live. May my meditation be pleasing to him; and I rejoice in the Lord." (vs 33-34)

Personal Response
Remember the text

Meditation has become absolutely necessary for me. I hope satisfying strength through Psalms will continue to lift me up. The author of the 'word' is my source of strength. I praise His name for the blessing I have received. I ask for encouragement and he provides the enablement.

Pondering Thoughts
Reflect on the text

Satisfying Strength has continued my Pastoral Health Care book series. My wife and I wrote it together as I went through cancer, open heart surgery and other internal issues. This included all the ups and downs during sickness. The last suffering was when she was killed and I got messed up in a car accident. This brought on spiritual, psychological and physiological problems. The meditation model brought strength through glorifying God and blessings.

Practical Application
Respond to the text

The experience has allowed me to be teaching pastor at a memory-loss center. It has opened many other opportunities in visitation Bible studies. It has used my Satisfying Strength as a source to deal with difficult situations in life. We rejoice watching God work in our lives. Psalm 104 is a hymn of celebrating the greatness of the Creator and creation.

Acts

PSALM 105:1-45

Primary Text

Repeat the text

"Give thanks to the Lord, call on his name; make known among the nations what he has done. Sing to him, sing praise to him; tell of all his wonderful acts." (vs 1-2).

Personal Response

Remember the text

I am thankful to God for His wonderful acts. I have searched for answers to assist me in my sickness, pain and uncertainty. It has helped me to deal with the outward situations. The most important part was looking onward to God himself. When I glorify God he blesses me. I have been able to experience God's restoration. It is God's wonderful act.

Pondering Thoughts
Reflect on the text

God's wonderful acts have been shared in my writing. It has been a means to glorify God through introducing me to a publisher, graphic designer, typist and adviser. Creative ideas have come to my heart and mind. Each group setting has been helpful and each group has encouraged others.

Practical Application
Respond to the text

New wonderful acts of God have been provided through small church pastors using the book series, a foundation to sponsor book gifts, and bookstore distribution. Psalm 105 focuses on the covenant (vs 8-10). God works out his divine purpose in human history. We live on promises fulfilled (Hebrews 6:12).

Remember

PSALM 106:1-48

Primary Text

Repeat the text

"Give thanks to the Lord, for he is good; his love endures forever. Remember me, O Lord, when you show favor to your people . . ." (vs 1, 4)

Personal Response

Remember the text

In writing my books, I am always thankful to the Lord. He seems to always give me ideas that work to help me and others. His love provides the motivation to win. Every meditation has brought enlightenment to my soul. The knowledge has brought strength to endure.

Pondering Thoughts
Reflect on the text

I know God remembers me. He knows all things. His love helps me to succeed. My faith is the decision process and hope is my expectation. I have become a dynamic disciple. I have grown in His word.

Practical Application
Respond to the text

This psalm is not to condemn Israel but to extol the Lord for His longsuffering and mercy. God shows his mercy against the repeated disobedience. We can see God's kindness and faithfulness in His sinful people. I am thankful for my life. I am thankful for His love. I am thankful that He will remember me. I can show His favor in my life because of what he has done.

Thanksgiving
PSALM 107:1-43

Primary Text
Repeat the text

"Give thanks to the Lord, for he is good; his love endures forever. Let the redeemed of the Lord say so." (vs 1-2).

Personal Response
Remember the text

Evidence of God's love is seen in these verses: "Give thanks to the Lord — his love endures" (v. 1). "Let them give thanks to the Lord for his unfailing love" (v. 8). "Let them give thanks to the Lord for his unfailing love" (v. 15). "Let them give thanks to the lord for his unfailing love" (v. 21). "Let them give thanks to the Lord for his unfailing love and his wonderful deeds for men" (v. 31).

Pondering Thoughts
Reflect on the text

These psalms are not quoted in the New Testament, God provides parallels in Jesus Christ. Jesus gives bread in the wilderness (Matthew 14:13-21), releases prisoners (Luke 4:18), heals and forgives (Mark 2:10-12), and calms the sea (Mark 4:39).

Practical Application
Respond to the text

The story of the 'redeemed' is the account of release from captivity, and thanksgiving is given. "Let them sacrifice thank offerings and tell of his works with songs of joy (v. 22). I accepted Jesus Christ as my savior and Lord at seven years of age. Discovering God's favor shares my faith journey. Growing in God's presence has been my joy.

Respect

PSALM 111:1-10

Primary Text

Repeat the text

"The fear of the Lord is the beginning of wisdom; all who follow his precepts have good understanding. To him belongs eternal praise." (v. 10)

Personal response

Remember the text

God's works are a reflection of his character, and his character is "gracious and compassionate." (Psalm 111:4). This means that "the works of his hands are faithful and just; all his precepts are trustworthy." (Psalm 111:7). Biblical ethics describe individual character as a single piece. Our innermost part is the heart. Our outward actions betray our innermost desire.

Pondering thoughts
Reflect on the text

"The fear of the Lord is the beginning of wisdom." (Proverbs 1:7, 9:10, Ecclesiastes 1:16). Fear has to do with respect (Exodus 9:30). It has to do with awe. It is a reverent understanding of God's powers. Fear and wisdom begins with God (Psalm 34:11-14, Deuteronomy 17:18-20). Wisdom is insight and discerning God's word.

Practical Application
Respond to the text

If we follow God's precepts, we will understand. Understanding is comprehending God's mind. Fear and wisdom will be a result of obeying the commands of God — His word is dependable. "They are steadfast forever and ever, done in faithfulness and uprightness." (Psalm 111:8).

Praise
PSALM 113: 1-9

Primary Text
Repeat the text

"Praise the Lord, O servants of the Lord. Praise the name of the Lord." (v. 1)

Personal response
Remember the text

This phrase translates the Hebrew "hallelujah." Psalms is a meditation book. We are to praise God "now and forevermore" (Psalm 113:2-3). The word "forevermore" is an eternal note of praise. There is no god higher than the heavens and supreme over the nations like our God (Psalm 113:4) God's sovereignty is not compromised. He is to be praised.

Pondering Thoughts
Reflect on the text

God is sovereign in heaven and on the earth. This means that God reigns and rules over all aspects of his creation. The Lord's sovereignty encompasses human affairs, especially the suffering of God's people. "Who is like the Lord our God, the one who sits enthroned on high . . . " (v. 5) I love the words "on high." God "stoops down" to help me and you but is still sovereign.

Practical Application
Respond to the text

God's greatest demonstration of grace was when He died for us on the cross. He condescended to become like us that we might become like Him (1 Corinthians 1:26-29, Ephesians 2:1-10). There can be no greater love (John 15:13). No matter how dark the day or impossible the circumstances, our God is able to do the impossible (Ephesians 3:19-20).

Call

PSALM 116:1-19

Primary Text

Repeat the text

"He turned his ear to me. I will call on him as long as I live." (v. 2)

Personal Response

Remember the text

This psalm is very personal, with I, my and me used over thirty times. I would like to respond to those personal words. "I love the Lord" (v. 1). "I will call on him" (v. 2). "I was overcome" (v. 3). "I was in great need" (v. 6). "I believe" (v. 10). "How can I repay the Lord?" (v. 12). "I will fulfill my vows" (v. 14). "I am your servant" (v. 16). "I will sacrifice a thank offering" (v. 17).

Pondering Thoughts
Reflect on the text

"He heard my cry" (v. 1). "Be at rest, my soul" (v. 7). "Lord has delivered my soul" (v. 8). "In my dismay" (v. 11). "Delivered my eyes from tears" (v. 8). "Delivered my feet from stumbling" (v. 8).

Practical Application
Respond to the text

"He turned his ear to me" (v. 2). "Death entangled me" (v. 3). "O Lord, save me" (v. 4). "You have freed me" (v. 16). God's Son is precious to the Father and to all believers (1 Peter 2:4-7). Let's end well and be faithful to the Lord (2 Timothy 4:6-8).

Faithful

PSALM 117:1-2

Primary Text
Repeat the text

"Praise the Lord, all you nations; extol him, all you people. For great is his love toward us, and the faithfulness of the Lord endures forever. Praise the Lord." (vs 1-2).

Personal Response
Remember the text

We need to praise the Lord like the early church. "Praise God and enjoying the favor of all the people. And the Lord added to their number daily those who were being saved." (Acts 2:47). We need to dedicate ourselves to worshiping God and fellowship with others.

Pondering Thoughts
Reflect on the text

"All you nations" (v. 1). The word "nations" refers to diverse nationalities (Rev. 7:9). We need to carry the gospel to the whole world (Acts 13:47). Sharing is our responsibility. "For we cannot but speak the things which we have seen and heard (Acts 4:20).

Practical Application
Respond to the text

We depend on God's love. We have been provided with divine assurance. We depend on God's faithfulness. He is faithful to help us. "The one who calls you is faithful and he will do it." (1 Thessalonians 5:24).

Revelation

PSALM 119:1-8

Primary Text

Repeat the text

"Blessed are they who keep his statutes and seek him with all their heart." (v. 2)

Personal Response

Remember the text

The two words "law" and "statutes" refer to the revelation of God. The Word of God helps us to develop a relationship with deity. It gives strength in persecutions and pressure. God's revelation is found in these words: law-testimony, precept-statutes, commandments-judgement and promise-word. We will learn to obey as we study His revelation in faith.

Pondering Thoughts
Reflect on the text

We must seek God, which means to hear his voice in his word. When we seek, we will experience delight. When we seek, we will surrender our wills to him. When we seek, we will have an appetite for more of his word. When we seek, we will treasure his heart.

Practical Application
Respond to the text

His revelation is my passion. His revelation is dependable. His revelation is illuminating. His revelation is joy.

"Let all those that seek thee rejoice and be glad in thee; let God be magnified." (Psalm 70:4).

Obey
PSALM 119:9-16

Primary text
Repeat the text

"I will obey your decrees." (v. 8). "I seek you with all my heart." (v. 10).

Personal Response
Remember the text

The Word of God is the most important book we have. It is because it is the revelation of God — who is the Creator (Genesis 1:1). We must meditate on it (v. 15). We must delight in it (v. 16). We must memorize it (v. 11).

Pondering Thoughts
Reflect on the text

I am able to obey with a pure heart (v. 9). I am able to obey with an energetic mind (v. 10). I am able to obey with an inner acceptance (v. 11). I am able to obey with intense instruction.

Practical Application
Respond to the text

"I will not neglect your word" (v. 16). It works for me. I will not stray from it (v. 10). "Praise be to you, O Lord" (v. 12). God gives guidance in His promises. I rejoice in them (v. 14).

Slander

PSALM 119:17-24

Primary Text
Repeat the text

"Though rulers sit together and slander me, your servant will meditate on your decrees." (v. 23).

Personal Response
Remember the text

Servants are persecuted and opposed. They stand against apostasy and hostility. They face trouble within and without. They face ungodly degenerate race. Meditation is one successful way to win. "Speak, Lord, for your servant is listening." (1 Samuel 3:9).

Pondering Thoughts
Reflect on the text

"Open my eyes, that I may see wonderful things in your law." (v. 18). The servant is a student. His manual is the word of God. God is the teacher. He will open our eyes (Ephesians 1:17-18). All we have to do is ask.

Practical Application
Respond to the text

This is my prayer: "Open my eyes." (v. 18). "Don't hide from me." (v. 19). Feed my longing (v. 20). Take care of the enemy (v. 21). Remove from me the enemy (v. 22). "Your statutes are my counselors." (v. 24).

Preserve
PSALM 119:25-32

Primary Text
Repeat the text

"I am laid low in the dust; preserve my life according to your word." (v. 25).

Personal Response
Remember the text

The word "dust" refers to my old nature. Sin, disobedience, falsehood, deceitfulness and depression. It is an inward look at self. God gives us an answer: "preserve my life according to your word." (v. 25). "For the word of God is living and active." (Hebrews 4:12).

Pondering Thoughts
Reflect on the text

God looks *downward* to preserve us through his word. He will teach us (v. 26). His instruction will provide steadfastness. His strength will provide security. His graciousness will provide sufficiency.

Practical Application
Respond to the text

God's word will work. It is a dependable source. Let's praise God for His word. His word has paved the way to success. Look upward and do what He says. "I recounted my ways and you answered me." (v. 26). This gives me correction. "Let me understand the teaching of your precepts." (v. 27). This gives me confidence. "I will meditate on your wonders." (v. 27). This gives me commitment. "I have chosen the way of truth." (v. 30). This gives me freedom. "I run in the path of your commands." (v. 32). This gives me victory. It is all possible through God's word.

Instruction

PSALM 119:33-40

Primary Text

Repeat the text

"Direct me in the path of your commands, for there I find delight." (v. 35)

Personal Response

Remember the text

This text is a key to Psalms. A leading feature is 'praise the law.' It is to give steadfastness in the midst of an ungodly, degenerate race full of trouble. The challenge is to end life well — "Teach me . . . keep me." (v. 33).

Pondering Thoughts
Reflect on the text

We have to put "teach me" with "give me understanding." (vs 33, 34). The will gives inner illumination. The balance must take place — spiritual enlightenment and obedience.

We have to please Jesus (John 8:29). We have to delight in Him (v. 36). We have to become selfless (v. 36). We must conquer a double mind (James 1:5-8).

Practical Application
Respond to the text

"Preserve my life" (vs 37, 40). My preservation is God's word. "Heaven and earth will pass away, but my words will never pass away." (Matthew 24:35). "All scripture in inspired by God . . . " (2 Timothy 3:16-17). The word 'inspired' literally means "God-breathed." It means breathing out of God. It is a product of divine in-breathing into its human authors. It is a divine operation. This is why I accept God's direction through the commands. I am happy in following God's will through His word.

Love
PSALM 119:41-48

Primary text
Repeat the text

"May your unfailing love come to me . . ." (v. 41)

Personal Response
Remember the text

The basic Christian virtues are faith, hope and love. "I trust in your word." (v. 42). "I have put my hope in your law." (v. 43). "Love comes to me." (v. 41). Notice God's unfailing love in Psalms. "Oh, how I love your law." (v. 97). "I love your law." (v. 113). "I love your statutes." (v. 119). "I love your commands." (v. 127). "I love your promises." (v. 123).

Pondering Thoughts

Reflect on the text

"I love your precepts. Preserve my life." (v. 159).
"I hate falsehood but I love your law." (v. 163).
"Great peace have they who love your law." (v. 165).
"I obey your statutes for I love them." (v. 167).

Practical Application

Respond to the text

Love will be a part of my activity when I have a cleansed heart.

Love will be a part of my activity when I have a confessed conscience.

Love will be a part of my activity when I have a consecrating faith.

Thankful
PSALM 119:49-56

Primary Text
Repeat the text

"In the night I remember your name, O Lord, and I will keep your law. This has been my practice. I obey your precepts." (vs 55-56).

Personal Response
Remember the text

Your name Yahweh is full of power. It is eternal and sovereign. The word 'remember' is important. In Deuteronomy, you find it fifteen times and the word 'forget' fourteen times. Let's remember some things that have helped us grow.

Pondering Thoughts
Reflect on the text

"You have given me hope" (v. 49). I expected great things in my call to ministry at sixteen years of age. I am eighty and the events are in my book *Discovering God's Favor*.

"My comfort in my suffering is your promises" (v. 50). I have had cancer and heart surgery. I have received comfort through God's promises at just the right time.

"I remember your laws and do not turn from them" (vs 51-52). They keep me secure and positive. The Word of God has been my steadfastness.

Practical Application
Respond to the text.

"Indignation grips me but your decrees keep me safe" (vs 53-54). I have learned how to handle people that disagree with me. In peace, I stand firm in my convictions. University doctrinate defense is a good example.

"In the night I remember your name and I will keep the law" (v. 55). My passion and devout dedication is caused through God's name that shows his character.

"I obey your precepts and practice them" (v. 56) I study the word (law) precepts every day. They keep me alive. Practice has always been a part of my life through music and now my spiritual convictions.

Master
PSALM 119:57-64

Primary Text
Repeat the text

"You are my portion, O Lord; I have promised to obey your words." (v. 57).

Personal Response
Remember the text

God is all we need. He is our portion (vs 57-58). We have a spiritual inheritance in the Lord Jesus Christ. We are complete in him (Colossians 2:9-10). He is our life (Colossians 3:4).

Pondering Thoughts
Reflect on the text

God is our master. Loving obedience is the condition for God's blessing (vs 59-61). Our job is to do the Master's will. My responsibility is to hear the master's orders, remember them and obey them immediately.

Practical Application
Respond to the text

God is the person we need to know (vs 61-64). We need to love Him, hear Him, obey Him. Studying His word and talking to Him must be refreshing to us. It should be our greatest joy. We must fear Him. "I am a friend to all who fear you" (v. 63). "May those who fear you rejoice when they see me" (v. 120). God is our home (Psalm 90:1). "Lord, you have been our dwelling place throughout all generations." He is our shelter (Psalm 91:1).

"At midnight I rise to give you thanks for your righteous laws" (v. 62).

Good

PSALM 119:65-72

Primary Text
Repeat the text

"You are good, and what you do is good; teach me your decrees" (v. 68).

Personal Response
Remember the text

The word 'good' is translated as pleasant, beneficial, precious, delightful and right. God does what is good because God is good and because what He does is "according to His word" (v. 39).

Pondering Thoughts
Reflect on the text

"Teach me knowledge and good judgement for I believe in your commands" (v. 66). Follow God's precepts, promises and principles, and you will be in His will. The person of faith does not live by the priorities and values of the world. (Hebrews 11:24-27).

Practical Application
Respond to the text

"Before I was afflicted I went astray" (v. 67). "The arrogant have smeared me" (v. 69). "Hearts are callous and unfeeling" (v. 70). "It was good for me to be afflicted" (v. 71). God overrules evil and from it brings good (vs 67-70). Affliction can be discipline (Hebrews 12:1-11). With love God disciplines. Obedience will come through obedience in suffering.

Word

PSALM 119:73-80

Primary Text
Repeat the text

"Your hands made me and formed me; give me understanding to learn your commands" (v. 73).

Personal Response
Remember the text

We need God's word for all of life. God knows us better than we know ourselves and He shares this knowledge in His word (Psalm 139:13-18). The Bible is a mirror in which we see ourselves.

Pondering Thoughts
Reflect on the text

"May those who fear you rejoice when they see me, for I have put my hope in your word. May those who fear you turn to me, those who understand your statutes" (vs 74, 79). Are we a blessing to others? They need to rejoice as they see the light of Jesus Christ in us.

Practical Application
Respond to the text

"I know, O Lord, that your laws are righteous, and in faithfulness you have afflicted me. May my heart be blameless toward your decrees, that I may not be put to shame" (vs 75, 80). We must accept from the hand of God both the pleasant experiences and the unpleasant (Job 2:1-10; Philippians 4:10-13). We have the love of God to comfort us and the presence of God to encourage us. Our prayer should be:

Give me understanding (v. 73)

Give me hope (v. 74)

Give me comfort (v. 74)

Give me compassion (v. 77)

Give me meditation (v. 78)

Give me blamelessness (v. 80).

Faint
PSALM 119:81-88

Primary text
Repeat the text

"My soul faints with longing for your salvation, but I have put my hope in your word." (v. 81).

Personal Response
Remember the text

The waiting process is hard through deliverance from persecution, judgement for enemies and just plain endurance. God does share some guidelines to follow. They will work with patience.

Pondering Thoughts
Respond to the text

Hope can take the place of fainting. We can expect God's word to work. It is a dependable source. God's character backs everything up. Enablement is provided.

Trust can take the place of affliction and produce rest. Learn to rest in His promises.

Practical Application
Respond to the text

Faith can provide victory. Power and peace will be a result as we obey His commands. My hope is in your Word. I long for your promises. I do not forget your decrees. You will take care of my enemies. I will not forsake your precepts. "Preserve my life according to your love and I will obey the statutes of your mouth." (v. 88).

Anchor

PSALM 119:89-96

Primary Text
Repeat the text

"Your word, O Lord, is eternal . . ." (v. 89).

Personal Response
Remember the text

Change and decay is all around us. The Bible is my anchor. It is settled. It is dependable. It is rooted in history and speaks to every generation. It was the defense for my doctorate dissertation at a liberal arts university.

Pondering Thoughts
Reflect on the text

The Word is eternal — everlasting. The Word is faithful — promises. The word endures until the earth is purified. The Word is a delight — equips us.

Practical Application
Respond to the text

"I will never forget your precepts, for by them you have preserved my life." (v. 93).

"I will ponder your statutes — your commands are boundless." (vs 95, 96).

The Word is limitless, boundless, and immeasurable. My passion is the Word of God. It is my anchor.

Passion
PSALM 119:97-104

Primary Text
Repeat the text

"Oh, how I love your law! I meditate on it all day long" (v. 97).

Personal Response
Remember the text

"I have not departed from your laws, for you yourself have taught me. How sweet are your words to my taste . . . I gain understanding from your precepts . . . " (vs 102-104). All we need is a heart knowledge of the Word. We must allow the truth to penetrate our hearts.

Pondering Thoughts
Reflect on the text

God wants our spirits to be yielded to His.

"I delight in your commands because I love them." (v. 47).

"I hate double-mindedness but I love your law." (v. 113).

"I love your commands . . . I consider all your precepts right." (vs 127, 128).

Practical Application
Respond to the text

God wants our wills to be yielded to His.

"I love your precepts; preserve my life." (v. 159).

"I love your law and I have great peace." (v. 165).

"I obey your statutes for I love them." (v. 167).

I love your word. (vs 97-100).

I obey your word. (vs 101-102).

I enjoy your word (vs 103-104).

Keep

PSALM 119:105-112

Primary text

Repeat the text

"My heart is set on keeping your decrees to the very end." (v. 112).

Personal Response

Remember the text

"I have taken an oath and confirmed it, that I will follow your righteous laws." (v. 106). We must dig for the treasures in the Word. "Accept my word — you will understand the fear of the Lord." (Proverbs 2:1-9).

"Blessed is the man who finds wisdom." (Proverbs 3:13-15).

"We are God's building." "We have God's spirit living in us." (1 Corinthians 3:4-23).

Pondering Thoughts
Reflect on the text

"My soul is continually in my hand, yet I do not forget Thy law." (v. 109). Remember God's word. "... the Holy Spirit will teach you all things and will remind you of everything I have said to you. Peace I leave with you; my peace I give to you." (John 14: 25-26).

Practical Application
Respond to the text

"Thy word is a lamp unto my feet, and a light unto my path." (v. 105). Let's have faithful feet, words, memory and heart.

"Pay attention to what I say, listen closely to my words." (Proverbs 4:20).

"Do not let them out; keep them in your heart." (Proverbs 4:21).

"Seek first his kingdom." (Matthew 6:33).

Hallelujah
PSALM 119:113-120

Primary Text
Repeat the text

"My flesh trembles in fear of you. I stand in awe of your laws." (v. 120).

Personal Response
Remember the text

The fear speaks of double-minded men (v. 113).
The fear speaks of the need for refuge (v. 114).
The fear speaks of evildoers (v. 115).
The fear speaks of deceitfulness (v. 118).
The fear speaks of the wicked (v.119).
I may tremble (v. 120) but the fear that conquers every fear is the Lord . ". . . what can man do to me?" (Hebrews 13:6).

Pondering Thoughts
Reflect on the text

"Fear thou not, for I am with thee; be not dismayed, for I am thy God. I will strengthen thee; yea, I will help thee; yea, I will uphold thee with the right hand of my righteousness." (Isaiah 41:10).

"The eternal God is thy refuge, and underneath are the everlasting arms; and he shall thrust out the enemy from before thee; and shall say, Destroy them." (Deuteronomy 33:27.

Practical Application
Respond to the text

Our defense is the sword of the Spirit (Ephesians 6:17, Hebrews 4:12). God rejects the wicked (v. 118-119). The enemy will fail! I will respond to the sacred scriptures. My fear is of respect, reverence, obedience, love, strength and peace. "I can do all things through Christ which strengthens me." (Philippians 4:13. "Be of good courage." (Psalm 31:24).

Discernment

PSALM 119:121-128

Primary Text

Repeat the text

"I am your servant; give me discernment that I may understand your statutes." (v. 125).

Personal Response

Remember the text

God's people suffer oppression, while the guilty go free. We see abuse of power and authority. Accusation and slander is experienced. We need to remember the Lord and what he does for us (vs 121-122). This suffering has caused me to look at three words: discernment (v. 125), will (v. 124), which deals with me in his love; and wisdom (v. 128). His precepts have the answer.

Pondering Thoughts

Reflect on the text

Discernment:

"The Almighty giveth understanding" (Job 32:8).
"The Lord hath given me counsel" (Psalm 16:7).
"God's way is perfect (Psalm 18:30).
"He shall direct thy paths" (Proverbs 3:5-6).

Practical Application

Respond to the text

Will:

"God will answer" (Isaiah 65:24).
"Believe in asking" (Matthew 21:22).
"Ask in my name" (John 14:13).
"Call on me" (Jeremiah 33:3).

Wisdom:

"The Lord gives counsel" (Psalm 16:7).
"The Lord gives wisdom" (Proverbs 2:6,7).
"The Spirit gives wisdom" (1 Corinthians 12:8).
"The Lord gives wisdom, knowledge, understanding" (Proverbs 2:6,7).

Light
PSALM 119:129-136

Primary Text
Repeat the text

"Make your face shine upon your servant, and teach me your decrees." (v. 135).

Personal Response
Remember the text

Seek His face and you will receive blessing. "I have sought your face with all my heart; be gracious to me according to your promise." (v. 58). Seeking with the heart will produce a burden for the lost. A broken heart and a blessed heart can exist together.

Pondering Thoughts
Reflect on the text

The light of God's truth shines forth and brings spiritual transformation. "We reflect the Lord's glory, being transformed into His likeness." (2 Corinthians 3:18). "I have treasured the words of His mouth more than my necessary food." (Job 23:12). I experience God's love through His word (John 14:21-24). Obedience to His commands sets us free (vs 133-134).

Practical Application
Respond to the text

Seek God's face with all your heart — reflect God's glory — treasure God's word — experience God's love — obey his commands. This will develop spiritual transformation and God will shine upon us.

Righteous
PSALM 119:137-144

Primary Text
Repeat the text

"Righteous are you, O Lord, and your laws are right." (v. 137).

Personal Response
Remember the text

We can depend on the Word of God. His Word is fully trustworthy. It will remain. "Your laws are right" (v. 137). "The statutes are righteous" (v. 138) "Your law is true" (v. 142). Your statutes are forever right" (v. 144)

Pondering Thoughts
Reflect on the text

"Your promises have been thoroughly tested." (v. 140). "Though I am lowly and despised, I do not forget your precepts." (v. 141). God's word has been found pure. They have been tested of persecution and criticism. The Word of God is truth, the Son of God is truth (John 14:6), and the Spirit of God is truth (1 John 5:6).

Practical Application
Respond to the text

Building life on God's Word means to participate in eternity. "Build your house on the rock." (Matthew 7:24-29). The world and its desires pass away, but the man who does the will of God lives forever." (1 John 2:7). Practice God's Word and watch your faith grow.

Communion
PSALM 119:145-152

Primary Text
Repeat the text

"I call with all my heart; answer me, O Lord, and I will obey your decrees." (v. 145).

Personal Response
Remember the text

Learn to pray in the fire of the Spirit. "Pray without ceasing." (1 Thessalonians 5:17). "If you remain in me and my words remain in you, ask whatever you wish, and it will be given you." (John 15:7). Live every day with open communication with God. Communication requires communion. Communion requires in-depth understanding of God's word. Praying in the fire of the Spirit involves love. "Hear my voice in accordance with your love." (v. 149). Learn to express your love to God. We pray not to get something but to show God we love him. This is wholehearted prayer.

Pondering Thoughts
Reflect on the text

Learn to pray in the fire of the Spirit. This will include a sincere heart (v. 145). This will include an obedient heart (v. 145). This will include talking to Him (v. 146). This will include keeping His statutes (v. 146). This will include rising up and spending time with Him (v. 147). This will include hope (v. 147). This will include meditation (v. 148). This will include putting the enemy in the backfield (v. 150).

Practical Application
Respond to the text

I have the assurance that you are near (v. 151). I will keep your commands (v. 151). I have experienced in my personal history that your statutes are established (v. 152).

Promise
PSALM 119: 153-160

Primary text
Repeat the text

"Defend my cause and redeem me; preserve my life according to your promise." (v. 154).

Personal Response
Remember the text

'Revive me' is the key to this psalm. Give me life, lift me up and keep me going. "Redeem me" (v. 154), "preserve me" (v. 156), "I love you" (v. 159).

Pondering Thoughts
Reflect on the text

"The eyes of the Lord are upon the righteous and his ears are open unto their cry." (Psalm 34:15, 1 Peter 3:12). Jesus Christ paid the price for redemption. He represents us before the throne of God (1 John 2:1-2). In our affliction he represents us, intercedes for us, hears us and meets our needs.

Practical Application
Respond to the text

We must learn to come to God in Jesus' name (John 14:14, 15;16). We must learn to come with the help of the Holy Spirit (Ephesians 2:18, Romans 8:26-27). God in His mercy provides grace (Hebrews 4:16). We can trust Him in His truth (v. 160). He is the giver of life and strength.

Rejoice
PSALM 119:161-168

Primary text
Repeat the text

"I rejoice in your promise like one who finds great spoil." (v. 162).

Personal Response
Remember the text

In Psalms, I have responded to the phrase, "I will be their God, and they will be my people." (Jeremiah 31:33). Yahweh and Israel would be in a relationship together. There is a battle going on: evil against good. I love "I have hidden your word in my heart that I may not sin against you." (Psalm 119:11). God is the master teacher and the Torah (God's will) is the life-saving curriculum. God's law is the revelation of his love. His promises are the sustaining power of life.

Pondering Thoughts
Reflect on the text

In the text, "rulers persecute me," (v. 161), "I hate falsehood," (v. 163), "I wait for your salvation," (v. 166), "I rejoice in your promises." (v. 162).

Practical Application
Respond to the text

In the text "my heart trembles at your word" (v. 161), "I love your law" (v. 163), "I praise you" (v. 164), "I have great peace" (v. 165), "I follow your commands" (v. 166), "I obey your statutes" (v. 167), "You know my ways" (v. 168). I have your word in my heart and rejoice in it.

Positive
PSALM 119:169-176

Primary Text
Repeat the text

"Let me live that I may praise you, and may your laws sustain me." (v. 175)

Personal Response
Remember the text

Our Father watches over us and accomplishes His will. "He restores my soul; He guides me in paths of righteousness for His name's sake." (Psalm 23:3). I have come to the Lord (Psalm 119:169). In my childhood, I learned to be guided by God. He has built me up in faith and provided understanding.

Pondering Thoughts
Reflect on the text

"When he has brought out all his own, he goes on ahead of them and his sheep follow him because they know his voice. (John 10:4). I know his voice. In my teens, I learned to obey his counsel. I have received answers to His promises (Psalm 119:170). My times have been full of God's favor. I have developed a positive attitude because of God's word (Psalm 119:171, 172). I have praised God's name all my life (Psalm 119:171-172). He has been my help (Psalm 119:171).

Practical Application
Respond to the text

"And we know that in all things God works for the good of those who love Him, who have been called according to His purpose" (Romans 8:28). I chose his precepts (Psalm 119:173). I delight in His law (Psalm 119:174). In my senior years He sustains me (Psalm 119:175). I have not forgotten your commands (Psalm 119:176). I will continue to serve and prepare to serve in eternity.

Worship
PSALM 134:1-3

Primary text
Repeat the text

"Praise the Lord, all you servants of the Lord who minister by night in the house of the Lord." (v. 1).

Personal Response
Remember the text

"Lift up your hands in the sanctuary and praise the Lord." (v. 2). The next fifteen psalms are called songs or hymns. It means "to go up." To focus their minds on what the Lord had done for them. The three themes were affliction, protection and blessing. You can sing in satisfaction and in sadness. Our greatest responsibility is to worship. We will spend eternity in worship.

Pondering Thoughts
Reflect on the text

"May the Lord, the maker of heaven and earth, bless you from Zion." (v. 3). The blessing is singular. We must learn to share it. Receiving is a joy. Obtain the sense of God's presence in your praise. Affliction and protection will turn into blessing.

Practical Application
Respond to the text

If God never sleeps and our worship never ends, then the blessing will not stop. God looks at the heart. Do I have a pure heart? Worship is a privilege. Do I meet the standards? There is no time limit to praise and worship. Your inner being has to be involved. It starts with the spirit. It travels to the soul and enters the body.

Exaltation
PSALM 145:1-21

Primary text
Repeat the text

"Every day I will praise you and exalt your name forever and ever." (v. 2).

Personal Response
Remember the text

I will exalt the Lord because He is great (v. 3). I will meditate on His mighty acts (v. 4). The human mind cannot fathom God. "He is everlasting, the Creator of the ends of the earth . . ." (Isaiah 40:28; Job 5:9, 9:10, 11:7; Romans 11:33; Ephesians 3:8).

Pondering Thoughts
Reflect on the text

I will exalt the Lord because He is gracious and compassionate (v. 8). I will experience God's glorious splendor (v. 12). "God is good to all." (v. 9). He satisfies every living thing (v. 16). He helps all that call on Him (v. 18). God loves a lost world (John 3:16). We must proclaim his kingdom.

Practical Application
Respond to the text

I will exalt the Lord because He is near (v. 18). I will experience God's desires (v. 19). He cares for you (1 Peter 5:7). Let's keep in mind "ask and you will receive" (James 4:2). God hears us, watches over us and supplies our every need (Philippians 4:19). Let's exalt His name through our inward and outward self. "Your saints exalt you" (v. 10).

Trumpet

PSALM 150:1-6

Primary text
Repeat the text

"Praise him with the sounding of the trumpet." (v. 3).

Personal Response
Remember the text

"Let everything that has breath praise the Lord." (v. 6). Everything that has breath refers to human beings, an echo of genesis 2:7, where God breathes the "breath" of life into Adam. This is a summons to all human flesh to join in the celebration of Yahweh's coronation and reign.

Pondering Thoughts
Reflect on the text

"Praise God in his sanctuary; praise him in his mighty heavens." (v. 1). God refers to Yahweh. It reminds us that he loves us and he covenanted to save us, keep us, love for us, and eventually glorify us, because of the sacrifice of Jesus Christ, his son, on the cross.

Practical Application
Respond to the text

I appreciate the phrase "praise him with the sound of the trumpet." (v. 3). God introduced the trumpet to me early in life. I have heard the best trumpeters in different styles of music and have had the opportunity to be taught by some masters.

Acknowledgments

Boice, James Montgomery, *Foundations of the Christian Faith*. InterVarsity Press, Downers Grove, IL.

Evans, Tony, *Our God Is Awesome*. Moody Press, Chicago.

Falwell, Jerry, *Liberty Bible Commentary*. The Old Time Gospel Hour, Lynchburg, VA.

Gaebelin, Arno C., *The Book Of Psalms*. Loizeaux Brothers, Neptune, NJ.

Gillette, John F., *Discovering God's Presence*. Freeze Frame Publishing, Lowell, MI.

Gillette, John F., *Pastoral Health Care book 3*. Chapbook Press, Grand Rapids, MI.

MacArthur, John, *Macarthur Bible Commentary*. Thomas Nelson, Inc., Nashville, TN.

Wiersbe, Warren W., *Be Worshipful*. David Cook, Colorado Springs, CO.

Zodhiates, Spiros, *The Hebrew-Greek Key Study Bible*. AMG Publishers, Chattanooga, TN.

Community Visitation study sessions.

Memory Lost Center study sessions.

The small hand on the front cover belongs to granddaughter Aliya Joy Gillette

About the Author

Dr. John F. Gillette is author of the Pastoral Health Care and the Divine Dialogue dynamic discipleship book series. It has been helpful in struggles with making spiritual, psychological and physiological adjustments. His many years of Christian service include certification in education and ordination in ministry. His studies have been in Liberal Arts with a triple major and graduate research in religion and leadership. He earned a Doctor of Philosophy in Biblical Christianity and honored with a Doctor of Ministry in Leadership. He continues in writing, Life Coaching and teaching pastor with Pastoral Health Care Ministries. The pain and pen provide knowledge of God's sufficiency.

"The steadfast love of the Lord never ceases, his mercies never come to an end; great is your faithfulness." (Lamentations 3:22).

Spiritual transformation involves a believing commitment to authority rather than passive opinion. It is an internal change (1 Corinthians 5:17) based on Biblical Christianity.

More Books in the Series:

Discovering God's Sufficiency
Going Beyond Ourselves and Experiencing the Supernatural
Pastoral Health Care—Part One

Can anyone fix our troubles? The answer is 'yes.' How do we conquer our trials? We have to affirm God's intervention. We have to accept God's indwelling. We have to make some adjustments through God's illumination. We can experience God's power, presence and peace.

Discovering God's Love
Confirming God's love through the evidence of historical facts
Pastoral Health Care—Part Two

We can obtain strength to conquer through a knowledge of the 'Gospels' and receiving Jesus Christ into our hearts. The New Testament books of history give evidence of God's love. Through his love and faith, we are able to be strengthened, experience his support and become steadfast.

Available at www.schulerbooks.com/chapbook-press

Discovering God's Counsel
Applying his spiritual solution to meet difficult trials
Pastoral Health Care—Part Three

Dark days can be life threatening. We have to develop an adequate level of spiritual, psychological and physiological adjustments. We can live with confidence in God's sufficiency.

Discovering God's Kingdom
Finding a way to understand ourselves in a complex world
Pastoral Health Care—Part Four

Dealing with life, death, heaven and eternity with God's perspective is necessary. It involves a personal decision of belief, trust and faith. Knowledge and commitment will bring comfort and security. The eternal destiny directive will provide the way.

Available at www.schulerbooks.com/chapbook-press

Discovering God's Heart

Feeling God's heart pulse is our daily challenge

Pastoral Health Care—Part Five

We have to practice the principles in the pastoral health care meditation method. We can handle any situation through thinking biblically. The spirit, soul and body are involved. Therefore, a holistic approach has to take place.

Available at www.schulerbooks.com/chapbook-press

www.ingramcontent.com/pod-product-compliance
Lightning Source LLC
Chambersburg PA
CBHW070055080526
44586CB00013B/1069